Your Money Made Simple

This simple and straightforward approach to money is refreshing and easy to understand. The illustrations and fill-in-the-blank formulas allow you to find wisdom for your finances and apply these principles to your life. It is a great read for anyone trying to get a handle on money.

Mark Batterson—New York Times bestselling author of
The Circle Maker, lead pastor of National Community Church

Whether you're just beginning your financial journey or have been on it for many years, this book will provide invaluable wisdom. Russ presents simple formulas to help you figure out where you are and where you want to go with your money. His insights will help you get on the path to financial freedom.

Andy Stanley—author, communicator, and
founder of North Point Ministries

Your Money Made Simple is an invitation to start your wise-with-money journey. This book provides a systematic, step-by-step plan to help you determine if you are spending less than you make and therefore have discretionary income. But it is so much more! You will encounter biblical principles and thoughtful stories to increase your wisdom and change your heart.

Brad Hewitt—former CEO, Thrivent Financial

It has been said the best concepts in the world can be communicated on the back of a napkin—or in this case, on a flip chart. This book nails the best of both worlds—simple, concise, and easy-to-understand financial principles and truths combined with a practical, step-by-step application to help us all accomplish exactly what we want deep down: *financial freedom*!

Ray Hilbert—cofounder, Truth at Work

Because the world is so complex, we often assume the most complicated solutions are the best solutions. In his latest book, *Your Money Made Simple*, Russ Crosson skillfully, and with extraordinary wisdom, challenges that assumption. Although he has spent his entire career in the sophisticated world of finance and financial planning, Russ offers people timeless and simple principles that lead to financial freedom. The genius of Russ's "one key" is that it works for everyone.

Chris Holdorf—CEO, National Christian Foundation

Russ and Julie Crosson have lived and shared these timeless insights for more than 40 years. They work! These proven, practical, simple but transformative principles will lead to financial freedom and generosity. You will find rich direction that's clear, doable, and anchored in the Scriptures. *Your Money Made Simple* is a compelling resource and a treasure that will not only be helpful to you, but one you will want to share with others.

Dr. Crawford W. Loritts, Jr.—author, speaker, radio host, senior pastor of Fellowship Bible Church

Your Money Made Simple provides remarkable wisdom on basic financial decisions and straightforward principles that we can easily apply to our lives. This book uses a simple yet captivating approach to helping us determine if we are on the path to financial freedom. I heartily recommend this extraordinarily helpful book!

Howard Dayton—founder of Compass—Finances God's Way

In *Your Money Made Simple*, Russ Crosson shares his many years of experience teaching and advising couples and individuals on understanding and managing their money. Unlike other books on the subject of managing money, Russ presents timeless truths in a simple way that anyone can apply. I wish I had this book many years ago.

Kim King—author of *When Women Give*, attorney, Exxon Mobil Corporation (retired)

Russ has had a great impact on my life and my family. In this book he has effectively summarized what God has taught him and shares it with you. I recommend you use his "flip chart" method and gain true financial freedom.

Jim Reese—president/CEO, Atlanta Mission

In *Your Money Made Simple*, Russ and Julie Crosson have shared specific, actionable steps that young adults can immediately apply on their path to financial freedom. I wish that this resource had been available to me and my husband as a newly married, 21-year-old couple. But, even after 26 years, we learned new strategies that we can put to work in this phase of our life.

Marilee Springer—former deputy chief of staff to former Indiana governor Michael R. Pence

Margin: the space on a document we have learned to reduce to get more on a page. This might get you more words on your next letter, but a lack of margin will not equal more peace in your life. After 28 years in coaching, I have learned the key is putting your players in the best position to be successful on and off the field.

Utilizing God's Game Plan (the Bible) and decades of experience, Russ delivers for you the key concepts that will put you in the best position to succeed financially. He unpacks the fundamentals of your finances and delivers a set of easy to run plays that will bring you the victory of personal financial freedom. More margin—which means more life. Run well...1 Corinthians 9:24.

Shane Williamson—president/CEO,
Fellowship of Christian Athletes

Jesus made it clear: Moment by moment, we're either in service to God or to mammon. He made profound theology approachable in its simplicity. In *Your Money Made Simple,* Russ Crosson has made the often-complicated topic of money simple. For four decades, Russ and his colleagues have been the go-to source for workable strategies in the vital realm of biblical stewardship. No matter your net worth, there will be valuable discoveries waiting for you in the pages of this practical treatment of a subject that has most people more flummoxed than faithful. Give yourself the gift of a few hours with Russ and let him coach you into a new level of transformation that aligns with truth!

Bob Shank—founder/CEO, The Master's Program

Financial freedom. We all want it, but few people achieve it. Yet it is available to all of us, regardless of income level. Russ does a masterful job of taking the complex and making it simple. Starting with a solid biblical foundation, he leads us on a pathway to our own personal "one key" to financial freedom. You will be blessed by reading this book and applying these principles to your life.

Buck McCabe—executive vice president and
CFO, Chick-fil-A, Inc.(retired)

Russ takes a daunting topic for many, personal finance, and explains it in a way that is simple to understand. This book is straightforward and a great tool for those looking to be better stewards of the financial resources God has entrusted to them.

Andrew Cathy—senior vice president, Chick-fil-A, Inc.

I've known and appreciated Russ Crosson for more than 30 years! He has a heart for teaching and serving the Christian community and has decades of experience in financial planning and matters of stewardship. In this book, Russ shares stories and insights on why getting on the right financial path now is so important. Whether you are just beginning your financial journey or have been on it for many years, this book can provide a helpful overview of a planning process that many find intimidating.

Austin Pryor—founder and publisher, Sound Mind Investing

My grandfather was a small business owner who was a part of the greatest generation. He told me that "you don't go broke making a profit." *Your Money Made Simple* expands on this simple concept, which Russ calls the "one key"—spending less than you make and doing it for a long time. This book guides you through a simple, but not easy, set of steps to achieve financial freedom. The concepts are simple, but our culture makes it increasingly difficult to follow them. I highly recommend this book to anyone who is seeking peace in their financial life.

Chad Merrill—president and CEO, Fellowship
of Companies for Christ International

More from Readers...

Russ's biblically based financial advice has had a profound impact on how I think about earning, budgeting, giving, and investing money. It's shown my wife and I how to budget our finances so our family can live off a single income—a decision that continues to pay enormous dividends for all of us!

The writing and illustrations in *Your Money Made Simple* are presented in a style that made it seem as if Russ was sitting in my living room walking through his simple "flip chart" process of budgeting money. Pull up a chair and let Russ teach you too!

Burke—regional sales director of an ad tech company

In the world of personal finance, there are multiple pathways one can take to achieve one's financial goals. Unfortunately, many are so cumbersome and complex that only a select few people actually succeed while everyone else ends up looking unwise, foolish, and irresponsible. In his latest book, Russ shares the one financial key that will enhance your ability to build wealth and live as a faithful, wise, and responsible financial steward.

Carlester—senior vice president of banking

After being married for 19 years and failing at various budgeting fads, we had mostly resigned ourselves to the thought that "budgets just weren't for us." The simple-to-understand and logical approach Russ lays out in this book gave us the agency and understanding we needed to have a successful budget, marriage, and (God willing) eventual financial freedom.

Shelly and Jeremy—parents to four children

YOUR MONEY

Made Simple

RUSS CROSSON

HARVEST HOUSE PUBLISHERS
EUGENE, OREGON

Cover by Brian Bobel Design

Your Money Made Simple
Copyright © 2019 by Russell D. Crosson
Published by Harvest House Publishers
Eugene, Oregon 97408
www.harvesthousepublishers.com

ISBN 978-0-7369-7694-7 (pbk.)
ISBN 978-0-7369-7695-4 (eBook)

Library of Congress Cataloging-in-Publication Data is on file at the Library of Congress, Washington, DC.

Printed in the United States of America

19 20 21 22 23 24 25 26 27 / Bang-AR / 10 9 8 7 6 5 4 3 2 1

CONTENTS

FOREWORD
RON BLUE

The year was 1980. I was 38 years old and had just started a professional firm helping Christians plan and manage their finances so that they would have more to give away. I had worked on Wall Street and practiced as a CPA for ten years when God gave me the vision and calling to start this new firm. The Lord blessed me with my first client—a physician who wanted to maximize his giving. I helped him design a financial plan to give more than he ever dreamed was possible. There were two significant consequences of that first financial plan. One was that I realized there had to be many more devoted believers who would like to maximize their giving but just needed help and planning to do so. The second was that this physician encouraged his young son-in-law, who was a high school math teacher, to consider joining me on this mission.

The physician's son-in-law was Russ Crosson. As Russ and I talked about his becoming a part of the mission and vision that I had been called to, I realized I had no idea how to bring a new person into what would soon grow into a biblically based financial planning company. I advised Russ to read books by Larry Burkett, Howard Dayton, and George Fooshee in order to gain an understanding of the biblical principles of money and money management. God's Word contains wisdom for all of life and has more to say about money than any other topic. Russ read the books and developed as much passion as I had for this mission. With great faith Russ and his wife, Julie, left a secure job and many friends and family and moved to Atlanta in the fall of 1980. At that time, I also hired a person I knew from my previous CPA experience, Erik Daniels. Together we set out to help as many people as we could apply biblical principles to their money management.

Over time we developed a conceptualized approach that integrated expert professional financial advice with biblical financial wisdom. This approach was highly replicable and effective, and by God's grace we built a significant professional financial planning firm, Ronald Blue & Co. The advice we gave was based upon God's wisdom as revealed in His Word.

In 2003 I left the firm to start another organization that trains other people to do what God allowed us to create at Ronald Blue & Co. God, in His grace and wisdom, raised Russ up to be the leader of this organization upon my departure. Under his leadership Ronald Blue & Co. had tremendous kingdom impact and became the preeminent firm in the country integrating biblical wisdom with finances. In 2017 Ronald Blue & Co. became Ronald Blue Trust and offers wealth management services in addition to trust services based on biblical wisdom.

For more than 40 years Russ's competence and passion for the mission has never wavered, and he has provided financial counsel and wisdom to countless couples and individuals. This book is a practical "how-to guide," sharing wisdom gained through decades of experience. No one is more qualified to write this book than Russ. I know that advice without implementation is of no consequence. When you read this book, you will see that the advice is practical, compelling, biblical, and driven by God's supernatural wisdom. It has been my privilege and pleasure to work with and watch Russ become an authority in biblically based financial wisdom.

I pray this book helps you on your journey to financial freedom.

Ron Blue
Founder, Ronald Blue & Co.

INTRODUCTION

If you would have asked me a couple years ago if I would ever write another book, I would have told you unequivocally, "No!" However, Bob Hawkins of Harvest House Publishers asked me to consider writing a *how-to* versus a *why-to* book, which has been the basis of other titles we have collaborated on. As we talked about the possibility, we agreed that the marketplace could use a different kind of financial book—a book that is simple-to-understand and user-friendly. A financial book with pictures and diagrams that take the complex issues and make them simple. A book that is applicable at any age or income level. A book that distills financial planning to its essence.

This book you are holding is focused on Albert Einstein's maxim "Everything should be made as simple as possible, but not simpler." It is your money made simple, easy to understand, clear, and uncomplicated.

What could be simpler than *one* key to financial freedom? Why the focus on freedom? "Freedom" is defined as being exempt from confinement or constraint, having options, and feeling unrestricted. That is what most people are striving to attain, especially in their financial lives. The opposite of freedom is bondage, restriction, and limited options. I have spent four decades helping people of all ages and income levels find financial freedom. This outcome is achieved by focusing on the *one key—spending less than you make and doing it for a long time.*

The following pages have a similar format. Each chapter begins with ideas on how to think biblically about the topic (taxes, giving, investments, etc.) and then gives clear directions on how to determine your own amount for each category so that you can know if you are spending less than you make. The book contains percentages and formulas that work at any income level, age, or vocation and allow for changes in investment markets, tax laws, and so on.

You will also see a consistent diagram throughout the book that gives you a picture that drives home the concepts. My hope is that as you make your way through this book, you will gain clarity and much-needed margin in your financial life. I hope that the myriad of financial terms that you encounter—such as stocks, bonds, real estate, mortgage, 401(k), insurance, taxes, debt, and retirement—will become simpler and clearer in your financial situation.

I look forward to journeying with you to a place of financial freedom.

THE FLIP CHART

We had just finished teaching our Sunday school class when a young couple approached my wife, Julie, and me. They were new to the class, and it was obvious they had a question but were somewhat hesitant to ask it. A little embarrassed, the husband began, "My wife and I have some questions and were wondering if you guys ever meet with people to discuss financial issues?"

Smiling, and with a glance at my wife, I responded, "Yes, we do. What are your names? We noticed you are new to the class."

"I'm James Miller, and this is my wife, Emily," responded the husband.

As I reached my hand out to greet them, I said, "It's great to meet you both. We're glad to have you in the class. So what issues are on your minds?"

"We have a lot of questions about a variety of financial issues," stated Emily matter-of-factly. "I would like us to live on a budget, but we aren't sure how to make one work. We never really know what we have spent from month to month."

James added, "My employer has a matching program for retirement, but I'm not sure we can afford to take advantage of it, and if we do, I'm not clear at what level. It seems everyone else takes advantage of the match, but with our monthly expenses, I'm not confident it would work for us, and I feel like we are missing out. I also have some questions about income taxes. They seem high and out of proportion compared to our other uses of cash."

James continued, "We also feel we should be giving to our church and other ministries, but we can't quite figure out where that money will come from."

Emily interjected, "We also have student loans and some credit card debt to deal with that seems to always keep us on edge. It is so overwhelming."

"You guys do have a lot to think through. We would be happy to meet. What time and day of the week would work best for you two?" I asked.

———————————

The above scenario has played out numerous times over the four decades I have been in the financial services industry. Countless individuals and couples of all ages have reached out and sought counsel regarding their everyday financial situations. I often hear questions such as *Can I afford this car? Should we pay off debt first? How much should we be giving? Should I invest in the stock market? Can we afford to live on one income?* and many more.

What I have come to realize is that every situation plays out the same way. The couple or individual comes to our home, Julie and I pull out a flip chart (which is a whiteboard with a pad of paper on it), and we draw six boxes. Their age, income, job, and primary financial issues are all irrelevant. We always start with the flip chart. Alternatively, if a flip chart is not available, then we use a napkin or piece of paper—or really anything we can get our hands on—to draw the boxes. Why do we do that? Because the answer to any financial issue is uncovered when you understand there are only *five uses of money*[1] and when you know the exact amount of money being spent on each of these uses. The six boxes we draw represent your income plus the five uses of money.

The challenge we typically discover is that most people do not know what is being spent in each box. They may say they have a budget, but if we ask what their annual income taxes are, then they usually have no idea. If we ask how much they are saving, they usually give us a glazed look and offer some nebulous "I think about this much…" response. If we ask how much they will have in the bank at the year's end, they look at us with an expression that says, "No one could know that. Are you crazy?"

DEFINING THE BOXES

In the chapters that follow, I will unpack each of the six boxes in detail, but to begin, let's define each box at a high level:

Income: This number is money coming in from salary, bonuses, dividends, interest, rental income, investment income, partnership income, corporate distributions, and so on. Basically, this is any income that is or could be part of your cash flow earnings. It is usually equal to any income you are taxed on. I will cover business income in the next chapter, but for now, income is simply a total of *all* income you receive from any source.[2]

---

1. Used courtesy of Ronald Blue Trust.
2. It does not include cash gifts or tax refunds.

Giving: This category is any money (cash, credit, check) you give to a deductible charity, a 501(c)(3) organization (e.g., a church, ministry, or nonprofit organization), plus any amount given to a nondeductible entity (e.g., family, friends, or neighbors). This category should not be confused with gifts (birthdays, anniversaries, Christmas), which are part of your living expenses.

Income taxes: This amount is the total of your federal, state, Social Security, and Medicare taxes, which most likely are all withheld from your paycheck.

Debt: This category includes the amount you owe on credit cards, student loans, car loans, and so on. It does not include a home mortgage, which is accounted for in living expenses.

Living expenses: This number is what you spend to live. It includes utilities, vacations, car insurance, gifts, clothing, food, medical expenses, and so on.

Savings: This amount is what you are saving **each year** and is calculated by taking your income and subtracting giving, taxes, debt, and living expenses. It can also be called margin, surplus or extra.

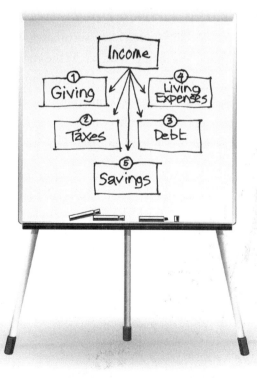

So there you have it. The diagram has six boxes—income and the five uses of money. It is that simple! Everything you do with money fits into one of the boxes, and the key to financial freedom is making sure the savings box is a positive number.

Freedom is being exempt from confinement or constraint. It is to have liberty and options, to feel unrestricted and independent. The way you find financial freedom is to *spend less than you make and do it for a long time.* This discipline will allow you not only to enjoy the trip through life but also to weather ups and downs in income or spikes in expenses. If you live like this long enough, then you can become financially free and have options as you go through life. This freedom can allow you to volunteer, take a different job, get involved in ministry, or take your pick from a plethora of other options because you do not need a paying job to continue to live as you have become accustomed to.

Let me take a slight detour here and explain why the focus is on "freedom" and not "security." "Security" is defined as being safe and free from danger or loss. Many people are looking for financial security, but that is elusive because there is no guarantee you can avoid all risk or loss and ensure that what you make or save is secure and safe. Stock markets go up and down, businesses flourish or go bankrupt, salaries vary, and real estate can inflate or deflate. Matthew 6:19-21 validates this point when it states that in this life on earth, moths and rust can destroy and thieves can break in and steal; only what is sent on to heaven is truly secure.

So while security is not obtainable, you can make sure that you are applying the one key to financial freedom by spending less than you make. At the end of the day, if you do not know the number in each of the six boxes, then you do not know if you are spending less than you make. In this book, I want to give you a process to determine the number in each box and challenge you to have a positive number in the savings box so that you can experience financial freedom and be satisfied. I know this process works, as I have seen it work in many lives, including my own.

Satisfied

In 1977, I graduated with a master's degree in education from Kansas State University. I immediately secured a job as a teacher and coach at a large high school outside Kansas City. I was making a whopping $750 per month. That's right…$9,000 annually. Over the next couple of years, my income went up, and I received a coaching stipend that took me to $15,000 per year. This amount was my salary when I began working with Ron Blue in the mission he described in the foreword and which I have been a part of since 1980.

Why do I share this story? Early in my career, I met a man making $600,000 per year—forty times what I was making at the time. The only problem was that he was spending $700,000. I remember walking into our apartment when I got home and putting my arm around my wife, saying, "Honey, the key to financial freedom is not how much you make but spending less than you make." We were spending $14,999, but we were spending less than we made, and that allowed us freedom and also put us on the path to where we are today.

I know what you are thinking. If you made $600,000 per year, then there is no way you would overspend. I remember thinking the same thing. Julie and I were on a tight budget; it was tough to make sure we did not overspend, and we had to do without some things. My initial thought was that surely this man had it made. How could you not spend less than you made if you made a lot of money? Unfortunately, a universal principle I have found to be true is that if you don't learn to live within your income at your current level, then typically, you will overspend as your income increases. For instance, this man spent $700,000 because he had grown accustomed to an expensive lifestyle, and he did not realize what he was spending in each of the five boxes. His cash flow hid the fact that when he filled in the boxes, he had negative savings, and as a result, he scrambled to pay his taxes each year and found financial freedom elusive.

What I learned early on as I advised people on finances is that if they spent less than they made, then it helped them learn to be satisfied with what they had. A satisfied mind is a mind at rest. It is content and at peace without craving for more. It is realizing that whatever you make *is* enough. It is deciding that whatever your income is and wherever you are on your financial journey, you will choose, as the apostle Paul did, to be content whether you have much or little (Philippians 4:11-12). As George Washington said, "We must consult our means rather than our wishes."[3]

Even when people are struggling to make ends meet or are in desperate financial situations, I cannot think of one situation where with some planning and review there was not enough income to meet their needs. It was not always easy, and in many cases, there was not enough for their wants, but they always had enough to meet their needs. We should not be surprised

---

3. Message from George Washington to Marie-Joseph Paul Yves Roch-Gilbert du Motier, marquis de Lafayette, October 30, 1780.

at this fact. God promises to meet our needs in Philippians 4:19: "And my God will supply all your needs according to His riches in glory in Christ Jesus."

So why are so many people struggling financially? I am convinced that most people don't know what amounts are in their five boxes. They may want to give more or have savings, but it seems difficult to find the funds. In this book, I will take the complicated and make it simple. I will break down the diagram Julie and I draw on the flip chart, explain the five uses of money, and give you some guidelines to follow. As you move through the book, you will be able to put your financial amounts in the "My Plan" diagram at the back of the book. I hope that by the time you finish this book, you will know if you are spending less than you make, experience financial freedom, and be on a path to financial peace of mind.

2

GROSS, NOT NET

In this chapter, I will explain what should go into the *income box*. This box is the most difficult to understand but also the most important because it is from this box that all the money uses flow. If this box is not correct, then you will not know for sure if you are spending less than you make. Before I dive into explaining what goes in the income box, let's first step back and look at how income is generated.

WORK

Work is physical and mental energy exerted for the purpose of subduing the earth (Genesis 1:28), providing for our families (1 Timothy 5:8), meeting the needs of others (2 Corinthians 8:14), and sharing Christ (Matthew 5:16).

Why do we work? First, we work out of obedience to Christ. From the time Adam was put in the garden to tend and cultivate it (Genesis 2:15) to the time of the New Testament, we are told to work with our hands (1 Thessalonians 4:11), and if we don't work, then we don't eat (2 Thessalonians 3:10). It is clear that working is close to the heart of God, and by working, we are obedient to Him.

Second, we work because it gives us fulfillment. We were created to work, and the idea of work was given to us before the fall (Genesis 2:5,15). We will not be fulfilled if we don't work and only live a life filled with leisure. Fulfillment comes from the *process* of working, not from the *product* of that work.

The challenge is that many times work does not feel fulfilling because our work environment is difficult. In Genesis 3:17-18, Adam had to deal with thorns and thistles. Today, we often deal with challenges such as difficult coworkers, unhappy customers, or technology glitches. But even if the environment is bad, that does not make work itself bad. To the contrary, it is an important activity that God says is good and a gift (Ecclesiastes 5:18-19). We are even told that it is fitting to enjoy our labor and view it as a reward.

For most people, the number that goes in the income box is money generated from work.

It may be an annual salary from a company, income from one's own business or practice, or an hourly rate paid for labor.

There are countless jobs in our world, and income is generated at various levels in each of them. Some of these vocations have a fixed income that is known in advance and can be easily planned for. Other jobs have a variable and less predictable annual income. These are jobs and businesses where variables such as commissions, sales, and expenses can cause your income to fluctuate, and you may not know your income until the year is over. As you will see in chapter 8, even if your income for the year is not predictable, you should know the minimum you need to make.

WHAT IS *NOT* IN THE BOX!

Recently I asked two people what their income was, and they both gave me the same wrong answer. They told me their monthly or bimonthly take-home earnings. That figure is not what goes in this box. This number is critical, as it is the starting point for all other boxes, and you must make sure you have it correct.

The reason your take-home pay is the wrong number for this box is because whatever has been withheld from your paycheck is still *your* money and fits in one of the other boxes! For most people, the following are taken out of their earnings before they see it: taxes (federal, state, Social Security, and Medicare), which will go in box 2 (taxes); retirement contributions, such as contributions to a 401(k), which are an investment and will go in box 5 (savings); and health-related expenses (dental and medical premiums, health savings plan contributions, and possibly long-term disability and life insurance premiums), which are all part of box 4 (living expenses). The key is to know that anything deducted from your paycheck is *your* money and likely belongs in one of the other boxes, most often living expenses.

WHAT GOES *IN* THE BOX?

Let's start with the obvious number that goes in the box, which is your *gross* income (not your *net* or *take-home* income). This number is your annual salary and your annual bonus. This amount is the answer I am looking for when I ask someone for their income level. As I mentioned earlier, if you have a fixed-income job, then this is an easy answer. It is a little more complicated if you are on commission; paid off the profit or net income of your company; or paid hourly and your hours vary.

If your income is variable, the amount that goes in this box is the number calculated in chapter 8. Skip ahead and work out the formula in that chapter to determine what amount goes in your income box. This is the *minimum* amount you have to earn to ensure you are not spending more than you make. It is your break-even number.

There are potentially some other income numbers to add to your gross earnings. You may have additional income from assets that make up your net worth. Your net worth is a listing of all you own minus whatever you owe (your debt).

Therefore, if you have a personal investment account (outside of your retirement account) or money in savings at a financial institution, then you will likely earn interest or dividends throughout the year. This income is part of your total gross earnings, but in most cases, such as with your tax withholdings, you don't see these funds because they stay in the investment account. They never enter your cash flow. They are already in box 5 (savings). However, depending on the size of the account, it could substantially add to your total income, and therefore it needs to be factored in to determine correctly if you have more income than outflow and a positive box 5 (savings).

If your net worth contains ownership in a business or partnership, then it is more complicated. In most cases, as an owner or partner in the business, you will not take out all the earnings. You may take some dividends or distributions, but usually, a substantial portion of the earnings are left in the company to keep it running. The total earnings and dividends need to be included in the income box even if you do not take them into your cash flow.

Let me illustrate: You are a 10 percent owner in a business that earns $200,000 in profits. So your share of the profits is $20,000. This number goes in the income box even if you only receive an $8,000 distribution. The other $12,000 is savings left in the company and is accounted for in box 5. The reciprocal is also true. If the investment loses $20,000, you need to show that as a reduction of gross earnings. Just like with dividends or interest on an investment account, you likely don't see the money because it stays in the business or partnership. It still needs to be part of your calculation to see if you do indeed have positive savings. If you own rental properties, then the same concept applies. Any net income (rent received minus expenses) should be in the gross earnings box. If expenses exceed income, then the loss also goes in the income total.

Notice I am not talking about appreciation or growth of your assets or business. The reason is that the one key to financial freedom is to make sure your earnings exceed your outflow. If you don't do this, you will never have savings to invest in building a business or to put in an investment account that can grow and appreciate and help you derive future earnings and thus experience more financial freedom.

Also note that retirement earnings are *not* included in the income box. Since these earnings are not taxable until taken out, they are not a factor in determining if you are spending less than you make.

What About You?

The income box is your gross (not net) salary plus any bonuses you receive. As discussed earlier, it also includes earnings from any other assets you own, which can be found on your tax return. Use the following equation to list these amounts and put the total income amount in "My Plan" in the back of the book.

Your Calculations:
Salary_____
+ Bonus_____
+ Interest_____
+ Dividend_____   } From Tax Return
+ Other_____
_____
Total to Income/Box _____

3

IT IS NOT YOURS

As we begin our dive into the five uses of money and determine what number goes in each box, let's look at a key difference in the boxes. Three of the categories are nondiscretionary, and two are discretionary. What do I mean by that? Boxes 1 (giving), 2 (taxes), and 3 (debt) are boxes that you are required to fund. They are not optional. You have to pay your taxes and debt payments. One could argue that you don't have to give, but as we will see in this chapter, God's Word is clear that as believers wanting to please Him, giving to His work and meeting the needs of others should not be an optional part of our spending plan just like paying taxes and debt.

Living expenses and savings are discretionary, which means you determine the amounts for these categories.

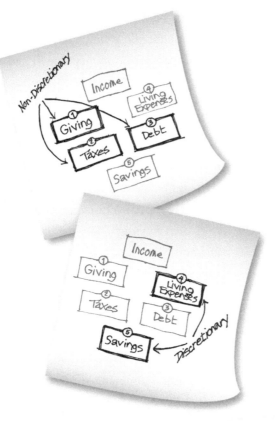

My Story

Shortly after Julie and I were married, we were working on our budget and determining what numbers would go into the five boxes. We figured out our living expense budget numbers, our taxes were set by the government, and by God's grace, we had no debt, but it was the giving box that caused the most conflict and needed the most discussion.

Giving was not modeled for me growing up. My family attended church, but we were not consistent or generous in our giving. What I recall was a few dollars placed in the offering plate on a Sunday morning. Now I was married, and my bride was sending monthly checks to missionaries all around the world! Not only did I not agree with the amount she was sending but I had a hard time understanding why she was doing it. Plus, how were we going to provide and make ends meet if we gave away our money? It was an emotional issue for me, and I thought that surely God did not expect me to give and at the same time take care of my family. How was I going to get ahead?

In counseling people over the years, I have found we were not alone. Being aligned on whether you should give and what amount you should give can be a challenge. Different backgrounds, temperaments, and perspectives on money can all make this area of money management a difficult one to agree on.

Julie had grown up in a strong Christian family, and as a result, she already realized the importance of giving. She knew what the Bible had to say on this topic, and I had to catch up. As I grew in my understanding of God's perspective on giving, I came to realize it was not only nondiscretionary, but to the contrary, there were a lot of powerful reasons to give. It also seemed that if I obeyed God in my giving, then the other boxes took care of themselves.

You may also think that giving is an optional or discretionary use of money. If money is left over after everything else is paid, then you might consider giving it away. Read on, and I will share with you what I learned; I hope you will see, just as I did, that giving is not optional, and it should be the first use of money, which is the reason it is box 1.

Wise Versus Foolish

To get to the heart of this issue, we can turn to Scripture. In 1 Timothy 6:17-19, we are instructed (many translations use the word "commanded") to be generous and rich in good works: "Instruct those who are rich in this present world not to be conceited or to fix their hope on the uncertainty of riches, but on God, who richly supplies us with all things to enjoy. Instruct them to do good, to be rich in good works, to be generous and ready to share, storing up for themselves the treasure of a good foundation for the future, so that they may take hold of that which is life indeed." The person who follows this command is considered wise. In contrast, in Luke 12, we read about the farmer who built bigger barns to store his earnings, was not generous, and as a result, was not rich toward God; he was called a fool.

You may be thinking, "Russ, that is easy for you to say, but the verse is written to those who are rich. I'm not rich." I get it. Everyone thinks that they are not rich and that someone else has more—they are rich, and you are not. But let's define rich. *Rich is having more than you need.* That definition fits most everyone reading this book. Of course, there may be exceptions, but in my experience, I have never counseled anyone who did not have enough to meet their needs. Maybe they did not have enough to meet their wants, but their needs were met. This should not be a surprise because God Himself says He will supply our needs in Philippians 4:19.

I like this modern-day paraphrase of the rich-fool passage in Luke 12:13-21:

> Someone in the crowd said to Him, "Teacher, tell my boss to pay the full, year-end performance bonus he promised me." But He said to him, "Man, who made me a judge or arbitrator over you?" And He said to them, "Take care, and be on your guard against all covetousness, for one's life does not consist in the abundance of his possessions." And He told them a parable, saying, "The stock options belonging to the manager vested after a major run-up in share price, and he thought to himself, 'What shall I do, for I already have enough saved to send my kids to college, my house is paid off, and I already max out my 401(k) every year!' And he said, 'I will do this: I will open an investment account and create a passive income portfolio, and I'll exercise my options and put the money there. And I will say to my soul, "Soul, you have a big enough portfolio to be financially independent; retire early; plan some vacations, play golf."' But God said to him, 'Fool! This night your soul is required of you, and the portfolio you've built what use will it be then?' So is the one who endlessly builds his net worth and is not rich toward God."[1]

1. John Cortines and Gregory Baumer, *God and Money* (Carson, CA: Rose, 2016), 120-21.

WHY GIVE?

Before we determine the amount in this box, let's look at six reasons *why* we give. The definition of *why* is the cause, reason, or purpose for something. Learning these reasons helped me get aligned with Julie and excited about giving.

Giving is a tangible way to acknowledge God's ownership of all we have. First Corinthians 4:7 asks, "What do you have that you did not receive?" The cattle on a thousand hills are God's, along with everything that moves in the field (Psalm 50:10-11). The earth and all it contains is His (Psalm 24:1). Deuteronomy 8:16-18 says that it is not the power and strength of our own hands that produce wealth, but rather, God has given us the ability to produce it. Giving acknowledges the ultimate ownership of our wealth and the provision of a sovereign God in our lives.

David understood this when he said, "Who am I and who are my people that we should be able to offer as generously as this? For all things come from You, and from Your hand we have given You" (1 Chronicles 29:14). Since God owns it, the right question is really not how much we should give but how much we should keep.

Giving is a tangible way to worship and show gratitude. God so loved the world that He gave His only begotten Son for us (John 3:16). God modeled giving for us, and we are called to do the same. Giving allows us to show our gratitude and appreciation for all God has done for us and is a barometer of our hearts. Giving is one area of the Christian life that cannot be faked; a person's checkbook or bank account shows what they value.

Giving is a way to show obedience to God's command to give. This reason alone should show why giving is not a discretionary use of money and why we should treat it similar to debt and taxes. The command is clear in 1 Timothy 6:17-19 as well as Luke 6:38 and Proverbs 3:9-10. When Julie and I were first discussing giving, I had no idea this was something God commanded and that giving was an act of obedience toward Him. Because I desired to please God, giving became a required part of our financial plan.

Giving meets the needs of others. Wow! I could not believe that the reason I had what I had was to meet the needs of others. According to 2 Corinthians 9:12-14, if we are overflowing (or have more than we need), we should liberally meet the needs of the saints (others around us). But the Bible also talks about the reciprocal of that. If I had a need, someone else would have a surplus to meet my need: "At this present time your abundance being a supply for their need, so that their abundance also may become a supply for your need" (2 Corinthians 8:14).

Understanding this reason to give has resulted in a lot of joy for Julie and me. We keep cash on hand that is already accounted for in our giving amount and wait for God to show us a need. It may be the employee at the dry cleaners, the cashier at the grocery store, the service individual at the auto center, or the server at the restaurant. Let me encourage you to use some of your giving box to meet the needs of those around you. We do not get a tax deduction on the cash we give in this manner, but the joy we have received from this spontaneous giving is priceless.

Giving results in rewards in heaven. The Bible clearly states we will be rewarded for how we have used and invested our money (1 Corinthians 3:8-14; Philippians 4:17; Matthew 25:14-29). Second Corinthians 5:10 says, "For we must all appear before the judgment seat of Christ, so that each one may be recompensed for his deeds in the body, according to what he has done, whether good or bad." Matthew 6:19-21 weighs in with, "Do not store up for yourselves treasures on earth, where moth and rust destroy, and where thieves break in and steal. But store up for yourselves treasures in heaven, where neither moth nor rust destroys, and where thieves do not break in and steal; for where your treasure is, there your heart will be also." If we are wise, then we will send money ahead to heaven (a safe place) and receive rewards because it will not burn up if it is stored there. The farmer in Luke 12 missed this point. He only stored up his earnings for himself and was called a fool.

How do we invest in heaven? We invest in people and encourage them to believe in Jesus Christ and grow in their knowledge and obedience to the Word of God. People and the Word of God are the only two things that last forever. We can give to our local church or missionaries, send youth on summer mission trips, help build structures, provide food for the homeless, pay rent for a needy family, send workers to help those in difficult situations, or fund Bible translations. There are countless organizations and opportunities to give of your time and money. I encourage you to find one that is meaningful to you.

Giving breaks the power of money. Luke 16:13 says that we cannot serve two masters, for either we will hate one and love the other or we will be devoted to one and despise the other.

We cannot serve God and wealth, and there is no freedom in trying to serve two masters. Giving allows us to hold our wealth with an open hand, puts God (instead of money) on the throne of our lives, and reminds us that we are simply stewards of all God has entrusted to us.

Jesus could have listed many subjects in contrast to serving God. He could have said God and *power*, God and *prestige*, or God and *creation*. But He didn't. He said God and money. Why? Because money is the one thing in our lives that we feel can give us all the things we want (and that God wants to give us)—security, provision, power, contentment, self-worth, and identity. The word "cannot" in Luke 16:13 does not suggest that we *might* be able to serve God and wealth. It says we cannot. No wiggle room! It is *impossible* to serve both! So how do we make sure God is on the throne of our lives and not money? We give. A disciplined pattern of regular giving breaks the power of money because giving becomes a natural and vital part of our lives.

WHAT GOES IN THE BOX?

Now that you understand why it is important to give, how do you determine the amount that goes in box 1 (giving)? Let me give you three principles to assist you:

1. *You get to determine the amount.* In the New Testament, there are no rules for how much to give. You are to give as the Lord has blessed you. Second Corinthians 9:6-7 says, "He who sows sparingly will also reap sparingly, and he who sows bountifully will also reap bountifully. Each one must do just as he has purposed in his heart, not grudgingly or under compulsion, for God loves a cheerful giver."

   It would be easier if the Bible gave us a defined percentage or amount to give, but it does not. You might be thinking, "But what about the tithe? Doesn't the Bible tell us to tithe, or give 10 percent?" In the Old Testament, there was a tithe (10 percent) for the maintenance of the Levites (Leviticus 27:30 and Numbers 18:21); another 10 percent tithe for the Lord's feast; and 10 percent every three years to provide for strangers, orphans, and widows (Deuteronomy 14:22). So 23 percent would be in compliance with the Old Testament, but we are no longer under that law; instead, we are under grace and the New Testament. So we get to decide how much to give.

2. *The amount you give matters to God, and He is watching.* Luke 21:1-4 illustrates the story of the widow's mite. Jesus was watching and took note of the rich people putting in their gifts and the widow who put in two small copper coins, which was all she had. He commented that it was not the amount given but the amount compared to what the person had to give. The widow gave more because she gave all she had to live on, whereas the rich people gave from their surplus.

3. *You are to give according to your ability.* Second Corinthians 8:3 says, "For I testify that according to their ability, and beyond their ability, they gave of their own accord." Acts 11:29 tells us, "And in the proportion that any of the disciples had means, each of them determined to send a contribution for the relief of the brethren." We can't give what we don't have, but we all have the ability to give something.

What About You?

What amount goes in your box 1 for giving? I suggest that you start with whatever percentage of your income you have already been giving. To determine this percentage, look at what you gave last year (to ministries or your church or to help a family member or meet a need) and divide it by the number in your income box. This calculation gives you a percentage that you are giving. Any money you gave counts in this calculation. It does not have to be tax deductible to a charitable entity. Approximately 20 percent of what Julie and I give is nondeductible, but it is still included in our giving box.

$$\frac{\text{Your Giving Total}}{\text{Your Income}} = \text{Giving \%}$$

If you have not been giving, then I suggest you start with 10 percent, not because it is required, but because it is an easy number to multiply and will give you a starting point. As we continue through the book and see what you have in box 5 (savings), we can revisit this percentage to see if it could be larger or needs to be decreased for a season. As we already determined, giving is not discretionary for a believer. Now, take your current percentage (or 10 percent if you don't have a percentage) and multiply it by your income number, and enter the resulting number in box 1 (giving) of the "My Plan" chart in the back of the book.

4

How Much to Uncle Sam?

He caught my eye, and then he ducked down an adjoining hallway. He obviously did not want to see me as we came into church that day. I understood why. I had worked with him for a few years and tried to help him determine the correct amount for each of his five-uses-of-money boxes in order to make sure he was spending less than he made. However, as a self-employed businessman, box 2 (taxes) always seemed to be an issue. It was April; he did not want me to ask about taxes. Most likely, he had not paid the taxes we discussed and would now owe a large amount on April 15.

He is not alone. For most people, box 2 (taxes) always seems to be a big unknown. At the end of the year, some people owe taxes, which is often upsetting because they have not planned for them and typically don't have the money to pay them. On the other end of the spectrum are those who receive a large tax refund and plan to go on a vacation or buy something with this unexpected bonus. As we will see, it is actually not a bonus and should not be a surprise. Before we look at how to determine this amount, let's look at how we should think about taxes.

GOD'S WORD ON TAXES

As we look at what God says through Scripture, it is clear we are to pay our taxes to the governing authorities: "Pay to all what is due them—taxes to whom taxes are due, revenue to whom revenue is due, respect to whom respect is due, honor to whom honor is due" (Romans 13:7 NRSV). When Jesus asked the Pharisees whose likeness was on their coins they said, "Caesar's." Jesus responded by saying, "Then render to Caesar the things that are Caesar's; and to God the things that are God's" (Matthew 22:21). As believers, paying our taxes is not optional. In other words, it is a nondiscretionary use of our income.

Many people think that their financial stress is caused by taxes and that if they did not have to pay so much in taxes, then they would be okay financially. This was the thinking of the man I mentioned earlier. He thought he would be okay financially if it weren't for taxes. He thought there were surely some creative ways to reduce his taxes, and then he could easily spend less than he made. The fact is that taxes are a result of your income. If you pay what seems to be a large amount in taxes, then it means you have a large amount of income. This can actually be a reason for gratitude if you think of it as a by-product of God's blessing.

For most of you reading this book, you should not overthink this box. Your taxes are determined by your income level. Apart from deferring them in a retirement vehicle, you should not spend a lot of time trying to reduce them. Not worrying about box 2 (taxes) should free you up to focus on managing your living expenses and increasing box 5 (savings).

WHAT GOES IN THE BOX?

The number that goes in box 2 (taxes) is the *actual taxes* you pay on the income you make.

When Julie and I meet with people and get to this box, we ask for their tax number. They usually hand us their W-2 or a paystub showing what amount is being withheld for taxes—but that number does *not* represent your actual taxes. Most people withhold more than they actually owe, which results in a tax refund. They may welcome the refund, but it does not help them determine if they are spending less than they make yearly. Unfortunately, the tax refund is often spent as part of living expenses because they think of it as a bonus thereby increasing living expenses, which makes it harder to save.

In many cases, those who are struggling to spend less than they make and have positive savings actually do have positive savings, but the government has some of their money and gives it to them in the form of a tax refund after they file their tax return. It is best to set your withholdings (if employed) or make estimated quarterly tax payments (if self-employed) that will result in no tax refund or a minimal one. It is also okay if you owe a small amount after filing your tax return.

So what exactly goes in box 2 (taxes)? It is your *effective-tax-rate (ETR)* percentage multiplied by your income. How do you determine that percentage rate? The following formula makes it clear and simple.

$$ETR \% = \frac{Fed + State + Soc\ Sec + Medicare}{Income}$$

Your ETR is the percentage of every dollar of your income that is going to taxes. For most of you, this percentage will likely be in the 10 to 30 percent range. You may wonder about those in other tax brackets you have heard or read about. What you may have read about is known as *marginal tax rates*. The way our tax system works is that as your income increases, then so does your tax rate. Some of the first dollars you earn are taxed at the lower rate, and as your income goes up, more of your income is taxed at the higher rate.[1] However, for our goals here, those percentage brackets do not matter. You only need to know your ETR for this exercise.

---

1. Sample Income Tax Brackets for Taxable Amounts

Rate	Individuals	Married Filing Jointly
10 percent	Up to $9,525	Up to $19,050
12 percent	$9,526 to $38,700	$19,051 to $77,400
22 percent	$38,701 to $82,500	$77,401 to $165,000
24 percent	$82,501 to $157,500	$165,001 to $315,000
32 percent	$157,501 to $200,000	$315,001 to $400,000
35 percent	$200,001 to $500,000	$400,001 to $600,000
37 percent	More than $500,000	More than $600,000

What About You?

This process differs a little depending on whether you are employed or self-employed. See the following for an explanation of both situations.

Employed individuals

To determine your numbers, you will need to locate three documents—your most recent federal tax return, state tax return, and W-2. Your federal tax amount is labeled as your *total tax* number on your federal income tax return. Your state tax amount is listed on your state tax return, which varies by state. You can locate your Social Security tax withheld and Medicare tax withheld on your W-2. Add these four areas and then divide by your total income. That calculation gives you the ETR percentage, which you then multiply by your current year's income. That amount is the number that goes in box 2 (taxes).

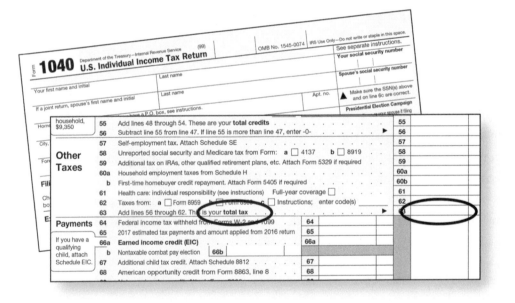

Self-employed individuals

To determine your numbers, you will need to locate two documents—your most recent federal tax return and state tax return. Your federal tax amount is labeled *total tax* on your federal income tax return and includes your self-employment tax (which includes Social Security and Medicare tax). Your state tax amount is listed on your state tax return, which varies by state.

Complete the following equation to determine your effective tax rate.

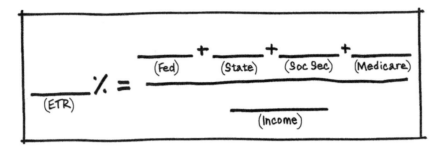

Here is one caveat to consider. If your income is higher this year than it was last year, then you will have more dollars being taxed at the higher marginal rate, which will drive your ETR up slightly. This is typically not much of a jump unless your income goes up dramatically. For modest cost-of-living and bonus increases, keep the prior year ETR. If you want to be on the safe side, then increase the ETR a percentage point or two. If you have a huge increase in income, then have an accountant do an actual current year income tax projection so you know exactly what you will be paying in taxes. This will give you an updated ETR so that you can set your withholdings or pay estimates accordingly.

Now multiply your effective-tax-rate percentage by your income, and then go to the "My Plan" chart and enter your actual tax amount in box 2.

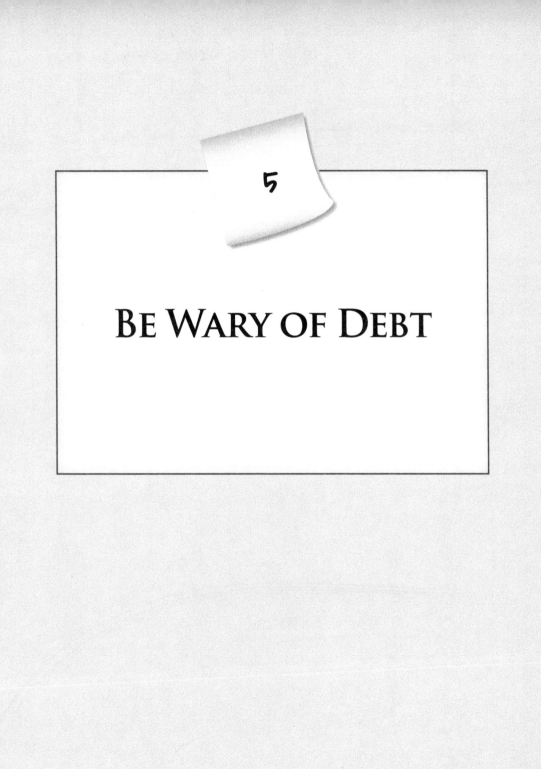

5

BE WARY OF DEBT

The client in my office had a very successful business that he had built over the past decade. As we discussed what next steps he should take, I mentioned that he should consider a plan to pay off *all* of his debt, including his business debt, over the next few years.

"You've got to be kidding!" he responded with an incredulous look on his face.

"I'm not kidding at all," I countered. "Your money may grow a little slower, but it'll reduce your risk; I'm not sure you can put a price tag on the freedom you will experience when you have no debt."

"I don't think I can do that," he responded quickly. "It would restrict my growth, and the debt is not *that* much compared to the equity in the company. My debt ratio seems to be quite conservative in my opinion," he asserted.

"You are right about your debt ratio," I agreed. "But you've no idea what the future holds, and even a small amount of debt can be problematic if the economy or your business changes for whatever reason."

"I get it," he smiled. "But I think I'm good where I am and will continue with the debt load I have on the books."

I wish I could say the previous story had a happy ending—that the debt never became an issue and the business continued to flourish. Unfortunately, that is not what happened. This man's business took a turn for the worse, and the bankers called him on the debt. Even though the debt amount seemed to be conservative, he could not pay the debt. He not only lost the business but also declared personal bankruptcy.

Before you conclude that *all* debt is bad and that you should never have any debt, let me set the record straight. The Bible does not have a prohibition against debt. What it does say is the following: "The rich rules over the poor, and the borrower *becomes* the lender's slave" (Proverbs 22:7, emphasis added). My experience is that people should simply be wary of the dangers of borrowing money, and as they move through life, they should prioritize getting out of debt.

Julie and I learned this principle early in our marriage. By spending less than we made, we put some of the savings toward paying off our home mortgage, which was the only debt we had accumulated. Looking back, we have no regrets that we did that and became debt-free in our late forties. We realize that we might have earned more interest or had greater stock appreciation if we had invested the money, but it was more important to us to avoid becoming slaves to a lender.

WHY WE TAKE ON DEBT

Debt restricts our options, reduces our freedom, and sentences us to a lower lifestyle in the future. So why do we take on debt? What are some of the causes, reasons, or purposes for debt? Sometimes there are legitimate uses of debt, and other times our reasons may not be as legitimate.

Legitimate reasons for debt include the following:

1. Starting a business
2. Purchasing a home / making home improvements
3. Investing in appreciating assets
4. Funding education

Illegitimate reasons for debt include the following:

1. Desire to keep up with those around us
2. Lack of contentment with what our current income provides
3. Wrong definition of success
4. Tax deduction
5. Current gratification
6. Presumption of what the future will bring

Let's unpack each of these:

Starting a business: Make sure the business plan is conservative and has a high probability of generating revenues sufficient not only to pay the interest on the debt but also to begin to pay down the debt. Resist the urge to grow faster by using more debt. It is wiser to grow slower and pay off the debt.

Purchasing a home: The key here is to put 20 percent down to avoid mortgage insurance and as a result not borrow more than 80 percent. Don't listen to the professionals, family members, and others who tell you that you can afford the payments and that you should stretch and get the bigger house. Look at the total mortgage debt balance and remember that is the amount that needs to be paid back.

Investing in appreciating assets: Just like with a personal home purchase, you should only borrow for appreciating assets, not depreciating ones. A rental house would fit in this category; your car would not.

Funding education: These loans are legitimate, since they will most likely result in higher earnings in your career, but be very careful with student loans. Only borrow what is needed for essential expenses such as tuition, fees, and books; do not borrow to supplement your lifestyle. Student loans are difficult to bankrupt out of, and the government can even garnish your wages if you do not repay them on time. Even though they are legitimate, I encourage you to be cautious when incurring them. Keep the total student loan debt accumulated to less than 25 percent of the projected starting salary of your career path. Note that there are ways to reduce the need for education loans and, if they are needed, limit the amount—perhaps live at home and commute, attend technical or community colleges, or take classes online.

Wanting to keep up with those around you: Much of our debt load is because we want to keep up with our neighbor. We want the bigger house, nicer car, latest technology, private school, spring break trips, or designer clothes. We allow the lust of the eyes and the lust of the flesh (1 John 2:16) to entice us to buy things with money that we don't have to impress people we don't even know or like. Credit card debt, supersized mortgages, and second mortgages are often incurred to try to keep up with others.

Lacking contentment: Unlike Paul in Philippians 4, most of us have not learned to be content with what we have whether that is much or little. The material possessions we have are a function of our employment and how God made us. We know He will always meet our needs (Philippians 4:19 and Matthew 6:25-34), and as a result, we should be okay with what we have instead of taking on debt for things we cannot afford.

Having the wrong definition of success: Often we buy things on credit because we have a skewed definition of success. We define success by the material things we have—our home, car, clothes, and so on. However, success is not about how much money we have or the "things" we own. It is defined as a favorable or desired outcome; it is to advance in growth or any good. Joshua 1:8 says if we do what is written in the Word of God—love our spouses, train up our children, work heartily, and share Christ with others—then we are successful in God's eyes.

Receiving tax deductions: Taking on debt in order to receive a tax deduction may sound crazy, but I have seen this play out time and time again. I remember meeting a man who was debt-free but took out a large mortgage on his new home. When I asked him why he did that, he said, "My accountant said I needed a tax deduction, and I can write off the mortgage interest." Wow! For every dollar he paid in interest, he got back 20 or 30 cents in tax savings (depending on his effective tax rate [ETR]). So he had 20 or 30 cents in his pocket versus the 70 or 80 cents he would have had if he had stayed debt-free and just paid his taxes. Don't take on debt to receive a tax deduction!

Fulfilling current desires: We should avoid borrowing to get what we want *now* and instead wait until we can afford it. We need to be willing to wait on God to provide our needs within our current income (Psalm 37). This patience will grow our faith as we see Him provide. I remember how Julie and I waited and saved for three years to buy the quality dining room table we wanted. It was worth the wait, we did not borrow to purchase it, we bought good quality, and we still have it today. Financial maturity is foregoing current desires for future rewards and benefits. Delayed gratification pays great benefits down the road and leads to more and more freedom.

Presuming what the future will bring: We take on debt assuming things will go just as planned, which is unrealistic and financially unwise. There is no guarantee that our salaries will increase, our investments will grow, inflation will stay in check, and our expenses will remain under control with no emergencies, ensuring we can pay back the debt as planned. We do not know what tomorrow will bring (James 4:13-15), so we should be conservative and limit our use of debt. Effective stewardship is about living within one's income today and not relying on the future. It is God's plan that if we borrow, then we must pay it back: "The wicked borrows and does not pay back, but the righteous is gracious and gives" (Psalm 37:21). Scripture also says,

"When you make a vow to God do not be late in paying it; for He takes no delight in fools. Pay what you vow! It is better that you should not vow than that you should vow and not pay" (Ecclesiastes 5:4-5). And finally: "For the LORD your God will bless you as He has promised you, and you will lend to many nations, but you will not borrow; and you will rule over many nations, but they will not rule over you" (Deuteronomy 15:6).

THREE TIMES AS HARD TO GET OUT OF

Let's look at an example that illustrates one of the reasons debt is so dangerous, subtle, and difficult to get out of. Let's assume you are overspending by $1,000 per year, or roughly $80 per month. Seems innocent enough, right? An extra dinner out or a new pair of shoes seems necessary and manageable. But if you do that for ten years, then you owe $10,000.

You decide it is time to get out of debt, and you are going to pay it back by paying $1,000 per year on the principal. Assuming a 10 percent interest rate, the interest the first year is also $1,000. So it looks like you need to reduce your lifestyle by $2,000. Or do you? This is where most people stop, but while the $2,000 covers the principal repayment and interest, it does not account for the need to quit overspending by $1,000 per year. So the real reduction in lifestyle is actually $3,000! So it is *three* times as hard to get out of debt as it was to get in it. The $80 per month was not so innocent after all. The following chart[1] depicts this reduction in lifestyle as the debt is being repaid.

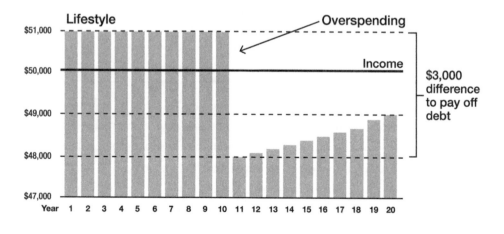

---

1. Adapted from Ron Blue, *God Owns It All* (Nashville: LifeWay, 2016), 112.

What Goes in the Box?

To determine the number that goes in box 3 (debt), add the minimum monthly payments on all consumer or depreciating debt (credit cards, cars, student loans, etc.) and multiply by 12 to determine the minimum *annual* debt payments. That number goes in box 3. If you are curious what percentage of every dollar of income goes toward debt payments, then divide this minimum annual debt payment number by your income.

You can use the following blank equation to calculate what percentage of your income you are spending on debt repayment.

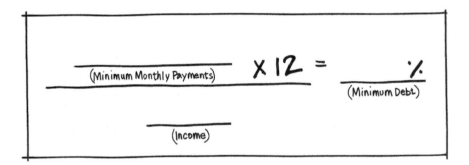

This calculation does not include your home mortgage. Home mortgage payments are part of living expenses, since the home is an appreciating asset and a big driver of overall living expenses—real estate taxes, homeowner insurance, utilities, upkeep and so on. Box 3 (debt) also does not include any business or investment debt, as we are assuming that debt is serviced by the business cash flow or by rental payments from the investments.

Someone recently asked me what a good percentage is for this box. The answer is zero! The sooner you have no consumer debt or debt on depreciable assets, the easier it will be to spend less than you make, have savings, and be on your way to financial freedom. One more fact: Just because the home mortgage and business debt are not in this box and are appreciable assets does not mean that they should not be paid off. Julie and I can testify to the freedom that results from being totally debt-free, including being free from your mortgage.

What About You?

Gather up all your monthly credit card statements, auto loan statements, student loan statements, and so on and find the minimum monthly payment due; add these amounts together, and multiply the total by 12. Then go to the "My Plan" chart and put this number in box 3 (debt). You may wonder if you should pay more than the minimum. We will discuss that issue later, but for now, we want the minimum number in this box. Remember this is a nondiscretionary, or required, outflow.

I hope that as we wrap up this chapter, the concept of *three times as hard* will cause you to pause when considering the use of debt. I also hope your thinking can become more in line with the thinking of generations ago. It is summed up best in these comments by Lewis Grizzard, a humorist and columnist in Atlanta, who wrote,

> If my mother had been put in charge of the nation's budget there never would be a deficit. She had some basic rules when it came to money:
>
> 1. Spend the least possible amount of what you have and save the rest.
>
> 2. If you have to borrow to pay for it, you can get by without it.
>
> 3. The secret to having peace of mind is not owing a single penny.
>
> Our parents took a lot of pride in being debtless. To owe was a sign of weakness. A friend my age said, "My father was proudest of the fact that everything he owned was paid for. I used to tell him, 'But you don't have very much.' He would always say, 'But what little I have nobody can take away. Can you say that?' I couldn't. As an adult, I never mentioned my finances around my mother. She would have been astounded at what baby boomers have been able to earn. But she would have been deeply distressed by the debt I have incurred. I once spent nearly six times what it cost my mother and stepfather to build a new house in 1956 for an automobile, which I financed, of course. I borrowed more money from the bank to pay for my house than my mother made in her career as a schoolteacher. But that is how my generation has gone for the good life. We borrow, and it doesn't bother us to owe up the wazoo."[2]

The sooner the debt box is zero, the sooner you will be financially free.

---

2. Lewis Grizzard, *Atlanta Journal and Constitution*, June 24, 1998.

LIVING WITHIN YOUR MEANS

6

Box 4 (living expenses) is the one that has the greatest influence on whether you are spending less than you make. As we have already established, giving, taxes, and minimum debt payments are nondiscretionary and have very little wiggle room in their payment amounts. Taxes are determined by your income, debt payments are determined by the lender, and giving is something you determine.

MAXIMUM AMOUNT AVAILABLE FOR LIVING EXPENSES

Before explaining how the living expenses number is calculated, let me explain how most people determine it. As Julie and I meet people, we find that they have a certain lifestyle (predetermined living expenses) that they are trying to maintain, and they spend accordingly, hoping that it all works out. They put this box first and hope that at the end of the year, they have not spent more than they made. They spend with no idea if their income will support their living expense level. As a result, they end up with credit card debt, owing taxes, or cutting back on their giving—if they give at all. They attempt to make the nondiscretionary boxes (giving, taxes, and debt) discretionary and the optional living expenses fixed.

To determine the *maximum* amount available for box 4 (living expenses), take your income and subtract the amount in boxes 1 (giving), 2 (taxes), and 3 (debt). This number is the maximum amount you have to cover your living expenses.

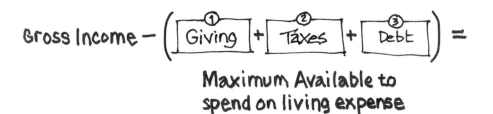

Complete the following equation to find the maximum amount you have available to spend on living expenses.

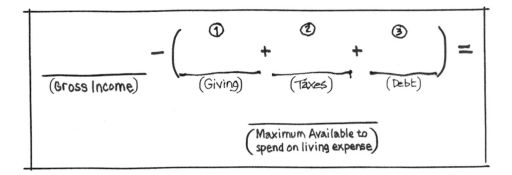

Once you determine this amount, the next step is to compare it with your actual living expenses on the next page.

This comparison will reveal one of two things:

Scenario 1: maximum available < actual living expenses = no savings = a problem

Scenario 2: maximum available > actual living expenses = savings

If you find yourself in scenario 2, congratulations! You have options and are on a path to financial freedom. In a later chapter, we will look at options for your savings. If scenario 1 is your situation, then you will need to take a closer look at your living expenses and make some reductions. Remember, the one key to financial freedom is spending less than you make, and this box is the only place you can cut. Before we look at some action steps, let's look at common mistakes regarding living expenses.

PRINCIPLES FOR LIVING EXPENSES

There are two primary mistakes people make when determining their budgeted living expenses. The first is unrealistically low numbers for certain categories, and the second is leaving other categories unbudgeted altogether. These oversights may be unintentional, but they can create a mirage that makes people believe they are living within their means.

Living Expenses

HOUSING	Amount Paid Monthly	Non-monthly	Total Annual Monthly
Mortgage/Rent			
Insurance			
Property taxes			
Electricity			
Gas/Heating			
Water			
Sanitation			
Phone/Cable/Internet			
Cleaning			
Repairs/Maintenance*			
Supplies			
Other			
TOTAL			
FOOD/EATING OUT			
CLOTHING*			
TRANSPORTATION			
Insurance			
Gas			
Maintenance/Repairs*			
Parking			
Other			
TOTAL			
ENTERTAINMENT RECREATION			
Babysitters			
Subscriptions			
Vacation*			
Sports/Hobbies			
Other			
Other			
TOTAL			

	Amount Paid Monthly	Non-monthly	Total Annual Monthly
MEDICAL EXPENSES*			
Insurance			
Doctors			
Dentists			
Medicine			
TOTAL			
INSURANCE			
Life			
Disability			
Other			
TOTAL			
CHILDREN			
School lunches			
Allowances			
Tuition/Supplies			
Activities/Lessons			
Other			
TOTAL			
GIFTS*			
Christmas			
Birthdays			
Anniversary			
Other			
TOTAL			
MISCELLANEOUS			
Toiletries/Cosmetics			
Husband misc.			
Wife misc.			
Laundry			
Pet care			
Haircuts			
Other			
Other			
TOTAL			

* denotes a nonmonthly expense

TOTAL LIVING EXPENSES

Sample Living Expenses

	Monthly	Non-Monthly	Total Annual		Monthly	Non-Monthly	Total Annual
HOUSING				**MEDICAL EXPENSES***			
Mortgage/rent	$1,200		$14,400	Insurance	$400		$4,800
Insurance	200		2,400	Doctors		1,500	1,500
Property taxes	250		3,000	Dentists		500	500
Electricity	110		1,320	Medicine	30		360
Gas/Heating	50		600	**TOTAL**	$430	$2,000	$7,160
Water	40		480				
Sanitation	10		120	**INSURANCE**			
Phone/Cable/Internet	225		2,700	Life	$100		$1,200
Cleaning				Disability	50		600
Repairs/maintenance*		2,000	2,000	Other			
Supplies	50		600	**TOTAL**	$150		$1,800
Other							
TOTAL	$2,135	$2,000	$27,620	**CHILDREN**			
				Allowances	$20		$240
FOOD/EATING OUT	$800		9,600	Tuition/Supplies	10		120
				Activities/Lessons	50		600
CLOTHING*		$2,000	2,000	Other			
				Other			
TRANSPORTATION				**TOTAL**	$80		$960
Insurance	$200		2,400				
Gas	250		3,000	**GIFTS***			
Maintenance/repairs*		2,000	2,000	Christmas		$1,500	1,500
Parking				Birthdays		400	400
Other				Anniversary		100	100
TOTAL	$450	$2,000	$7,400	Other			
				TOTAL		$2,000	$2,000
ENTERTAINMENT RECREATION							
Babysitters	$100		$1,200	**MISCELLANEOUS**			
Subscriptions	25		300	Toiletries/Cosmetics	$20		$240
Vacation*		2,000	2,000	Husband misc.	100		1,200
Sports or Hobbies				Wife misc.	100		1,200
Other				Dry Cleaning	20		240
Other				Pet care	50		600
TOTAL	$125	$2,000	$3,500	Haircuts	50		600
				Other			
				Other			
				TOTAL	$340		$4,080

*denotes a nonmonthly expense

	Monthly	Non-Monthly	Total Annual
TOTAL LIVING EXPENSES	$4,510	$12,000	$66,120

Unbudgeted categories: When setting a budget, one of the most common mistakes I see is leaving out important categories altogether. The categories that are typically left out are those where you don't know in advance what the expenses might be (e.g., car repairs, home maintenance and repairs, medical expenses not covered by insurance, and kids' activity fees). This mistake is critical. You should look at your expenses from the past year to estimate a reasonable number. A couple of other pointers to consider are as follows: 1.5 to 2 percent of your house value is a good number to estimate for proactive maintenance and repairs, and for auto repairs, start at $1,000 and increase the amount as your car gets older. You may notice that on the sample living expense sheet on the previous page, no categories are left out. It is imperative to account for everything you spend.

I received a letter that drove home the importance of not leaving categories unbudgeted. The letter read, "I have never really gripped the cost of day-to-day living. I sweep things like clothes, gasoline, dental expenses, brakes, and gifts in a little pile called incidentals. Well, it is not a little pile called incidentals; it is a big pile called essentials. Not only was the pile larger than I realized; the category was wrong." Once you get all the categories accounted for, then the next key is to be realistic with your estimated amounts.

Realistic numbers: Julie and I recently met with a couple to help them review their budget. The first number that jumped out to us was the amount allocated for food. For a growing family of five, they had budgeted $600 per month and never seemed to have enough money each month for food. My experience told me that they probably needed to increase that number by a few hundred dollars each month.

Often, people set unrealistic budget amounts to make themselves feel like they are living within their income. They think if they put in a lower amount to make sure all the categories are covered, then it will all work out. Unfortunately, a budget does not work that way.

The best way to determine realistic numbers is to look at your actual spending over the past year or so.[1] This research will give you a good idea of what should be budgeted for food, utilities, gasoline, and so on. Also, seeking comparative input from peers in a similar demographic and geographic location can add some realism to your budgeted amounts. Alternatively, seek out a professional advisor who can add another perspective to your numbers. If

---

1. If you don't have a tracking system, then that would be a nonnegotiable first step. Tracking gives you data to set a realistic budget. Take a look at www.mvelopes.com, www.mint.com, or www.youneedabudget.com.

you are married, then you will have a more accurate estimate if both spouses weigh in, since one of you may be closer to some categories than the other one.

WHAT GOES IN THE BOX?

The number that goes in box 4 (living expenses) is the lesser of the maximum available amount (calculated at the beginning of this chapter) or the actual living expenses from page 63.

What About You?

We are now at the most critical juncture of this entire process. You need to fill in the living expenses chart on page 63 with realistic numbers and be sure not to leave any categories out. Some of these numbers, such as medical and dental premiums or health savings accounts, are likely being withheld from your paycheck. Check your paystub to ensure you have included all these expenses as well. Next, you will compare your actual numbers from page 63 to the maximum number you have available. Then go to the "My Plan" chart and enter the smaller of the two numbers.

If you need to cut some of your expenses to bring them in line with your income and create positive savings, then the first place to start is God's Word. As we saw in the last chapter, one of the key reasons people take on consumer debt is that they have not learned to be content with the income God has allowed them to make. So thinking correctly and learning to be content are the first steps to bringing your actual expenses in line with your income.

Contentment: First Timothy 6:7-10 tells us to be content with food and covering and to be careful of longing for many foolish and harmful desires, which can plunge us into ruin. According to 1 John 2:15-17, we are to avoid the lust of the flesh and the lust of the eyes. And as Paul says in Philippians 4:11-12, we are to learn to be content in whatever circumstance—whether we have much or little. In Hebrews 13:5 (emphasis added), we read, "Make sure that your character is free from the love of money, being content with what you have; for He Himself has said, 'I WILL NEVER DESERT YOU, NOR WILL I EVER FORSAKE YOU.'" We can take comfort in the fact that the God of the universe will meet our needs (Philippians 4:19). He takes care of the lilies of the field and the birds of the air with food, drink, and clothing, and so too will He take care of us (Matthew 6:25-34). As you are wrestling with how to reduce your living expenses, remember what G.K. Chesterton, a British writer and theologian, said, "There are two ways to get enough. One is to accumulate more. The other is to desire less."[2] British historian Richard Evans also commented, "May we never let the things we can't have or don't have or shouldn't have spoil our enjoyment of the things we can have and do have."[3]

You might be thinking that although it is good to be content, what are some practical steps you can take? Here are some ideas of where you can reduce your spending to get your actual living expenses below your maximum amount available.

Groceries. Are you planning ahead for meals and buying in bulk when possible? Watch for sale items or compare prices available from warehouse clubs. Are you avoiding the pricy, individually packaged snacks? How much are you spending on coffee on the way to work? Maybe consider packing a lunch instead of eating out at lunch. Are you having groceries delivered? Those can be more expensive than shopping yourself.

---

2. G.K. Chesteron, *The Crimes of England* (Catholic Way Publishing, 2013).

3. www.goodreads.com/quotes/18764.

Eating out. This area adds up quickly, so maybe cut back or cut it out completely. Identify a number of times per month you will go out and stick to it. If you do go out, skip the drinks and appetizers, as that can reduce the bill by about 20 percent. Look for coupons or local deals, such as kids-eat-free nights. Consider splitting an entrée. Julie and I do this frequently and find we still get plenty to eat.

Phone and Internet. Do you have to have the newest edition phone? Consider buying factory refurbished or prior generation technology. For monthly cell phone service, consider switching to a low cost provider or bundling your phone, Internet, and cable. Do you still have a landline? Perhaps you can drop it and just use your cell phone. Have you price shopped your Internet service? Even if you don't switch, ask your current provider if they can honor pricing available from competitors.

Monthly services and subscriptions. Review all your recurring bills—such as cable/satellite, movie and music subscription services, and gym memberships—to determine if they are still valuable to you. What about lawn care or house cleaning services? Could this be an opportunity to burn some extra calories or help your children earn an allowance?

Insurance. How long has it been since you got a price comparison on your auto, home, life, and umbrella insurance policies? Price is not the only consideration. Sometime savings can be achieved while maintaining or improving your coverage. Consider working with an independent agent who can price multiple insurers.

Leisure activities. Look at how much you are spending on hobbies and events. Consider cutting back on greens fees or concert tickets and pursuing less expensive activities such as hiking or biking. Also review the cost of your kids' activities such as sports, lessons, or camps. Maybe now is a good time for them to focus on the one activity that they are most passionate about or to reduce the number of weekly lessons, thus reducing the cost for your family.

Clothes. Plan ahead and shop the sales. Consider looking for local consignment sales or secondhand stores, especially for children's clothing, since they outgrow them so quickly. My son loves shopping for treasures at Goodwill and as a result gets several nice items at a fraction of the cost. Try to buy clothes only if you love the way they look and fit. Otherwise, they may be relegated to a dark corner of your closet!

Vacations. I believe vacations are important, but they can also be expensive. Is there a destination where staying with family or camping might offer an enjoyable vacation at a lower price? Or perhaps you can consider a "staycation" seeing and doing things right in your own city? Driving and seeing the country versus flying can also save money and create memorable family experiences.

Gifts. Over the years, Julie and I have learned some great lessons in this category. First, you can save money by making gifts versus buying them, which we did early in our marriage when our budget was tight. But our biggest "aha" and budget stretcher came two years into our marriage when we went on a trip to Africa. We bought wood carvings from a local market at a very good value as Christmas gifts. The trip was in March. We came home and put the gifts in a closet. We realized two things. It was great to have Christmas shopping done early! But we also realized if we shopped early every year, we could buy more with our money. Thus the "gift closet" concept was born. Now we buy gifts for weddings, birthdays, graduations, and so on early in the year and put them in the gift closet. Julie and I do most of our shopping to replenish our gift closet in January during the after-Christmas sales. One year, we bought ten items for the cost of one. They were 90 percent off! You may be thinking that it is not very thoughtful to just go to the gift closet and pull out a wedding or birthday gift. We have come to realize over the years that no one in our circle of friends (and probably not in yours either) *needs* anything, and kids are happy to receive just about any birthday gift. Of course, there are occasions when a more personalized gift is needed, but our gift closet covers 99 percent of our gifting needs at a lower cost.

You could also consider giving experiences instead of material gifts, especially to your own children. For example, you could have an "adventure day" where your child gets to spend a day alone with Mom or Dad doing something fun. Or perhaps buy season tickets to a local museum or attraction instead of more toys or technology.

Home.[4] Many of your living expenses are fixed and driven by your home. The more expensive the home, the higher the mortgage, the real estate taxes, the utilities, and the upkeep. Even though downsizing is often a great solution to reducing living expenses, it is not the first place to look. Since mortgage interest and real estate taxes are deductible on your taxes, the savings achieved with a smaller house are never as much as you think. Secondarily, the cost to move can mitigate the annual savings for a few years, and you have to consider the stress that moving causes. Unless you are downsizing dramatically (reducing the mortgage by 30 to 50 percent), look closely at the numbers before taking this step. Be aggressive in cutting other categories first.

Autos. As with houses, the more expensive the car, the more the insurance, tag fees, and, in some cases, gasoline costs (if it requires premium fuel). The best rule here is to drive the older, less expensive car longer. The car you own now is the cheapest car you can own. Plan to keep it as long as possible. Of course, if you owe money on it (box 3, debt) then selling it and purchasing a less expensive car with no monthly payment is a good way to go.

There are many other creative ways to cut living expenses. Look for blogs and other resources to help you live more frugally.

The key is to take the first step. If you reduce your expenses now, then it will get easier later; I promise! Unfortunately, if you continue to live beyond your income, then it will only get harder later.

---

4. My comments here assume you already own a home. Know, however, that the home buying decision is the most critical decision you will make in that it typically commands the largest percentage of your income (25-35%). Therefore, my encouragement is to buy a smaller house and live in it longer to keep your living expenses down and savings up. I would recommend reading "Why (Prudent) Spending Rates Matter More Than Savings Rates" by Michael Kitcie (www.kitces.com, September 5, 2018). This article will offer some percentage guidelines for various living expense categories.

1

EVERYTHING GOES IN AN ENVELOPE

The doorbell rang at exactly 7:00 p.m. Ben and Elizabeth were right on time. They had approached Julie and me a couple weeks earlier with some questions about their budget. We were happy to meet with them to see how we could help.

"Come on in. It's good to see you," I commented as I opened the door. "Glad you all could make it."

"Thanks for having us over," Ben responded as he shook my hand. "Elizabeth and I have been looking forward to this meeting."

"Great," I continued.

"Could I get you something to drink?" Julie interjected.

"Water would be great," they responded.

"So how can we help you?" Julie asked as we sat down around the kitchen table. "We are all ears."

"I don't really know where to start," Ben began. "We just never seem to be able to make a budget work. We're always over in different categories each month, and by the end of the year, we seem to have spent more than we earned."

"And I never know what I have left for the kids' clothes," Elizabeth chimed in. "Not to mention birthday gifts and other expenses that come up, like when the kids get sick or need money for special events at school. It all seems so confusing. I told Ben that I would really like us to take a family vacation this year, but we are not sure if that is in the budget."

"We are hoping our tax refund can cover the vacation," Ben interjected. "But I am afraid that may already be committed to covering a car repair we just incurred. That is the issue. Something always seems to come up. We go paycheck to paycheck, and even though I make good money, the budget always seems to be stretched. We start every year with good intentions, but usually, by February, something has happened, and we are over in some categories; we don't know how to get back on track. We have tried a lot of different methods of budgeting, but nothing seems to work for us."

"Let me encourage you both," I commented as I pulled the flip chart closer to the table. "You are not alone. In all the years Julie and I have met with people regarding their budgets, the issues you mentioned are the same ones we hear time and time again. We are asked *Why can't we seem to make a budget work? Why do we start out okay in January but the wheels seem to come off in February? How is it possible to budget for variable expenses like car repairs?* Why don't we take the confusion out of the budgeting issue? Let us share with you not only the biblical basis for budgeting but also some principles, techniques, and keys that will make this area a nonissue. How does that sound?"

"Sure sounds good to me!" Ben shared with some building excitement as he leaned forward in his chair.

"I agree," Elizabeth chimed in. "I can't wait to make budgeting simple."

The theme of this book is *simple*—taking the apparent complexities surrounding money and clarifying them so you can have peace of mind in your finances.

THE BIBLE ON BUDGETING

The foundational Scripture on budgeting is found in Proverbs 27:23-24: "Know well the condition of your flocks, and pay attention to your herds; for riches are not forever, nor does a crown endure to all generations." In today's vernacular, this verse confirms that we should know where our money is going versus wondering where it went.

For the purposes of this discussion, we are defining the term "budgeting" as how people are going to handle and be intentional about their living expenses (box 4). I believe that this is what most people mean when they say they are "on a budget." They are referring to their living expenses. They are not typically thinking about giving, taxes, and debt. In the last chapter, we discussed how to determine your living expense number. In this chapter, we will look at principles, techniques, and keys to make a budget work and to ensure you are staying within the number in box 4 (living expenses), which is the key to financial freedom.

KEYS TO A BUDGET SYSTEM THAT WORKS

Once you have established your living expenses on page 63 in chapter 6, then it's time to develop a system to ensure you stay within your budget. The following are two principles that are common in budget systems that work.

Any system is in essence an "envelope system."

A traditional envelope system is when you store cash in separate envelopes to meet different categories of expenses. It doesn't matter if you use sophisticated software, a simple spreadsheet, or actual envelopes; the principle is the same. You decide what goes into each budget category—such as utilities, gasoline, vacation savings, clothing, gifts, allowances, or insurance—and you put that dollar amount into each envelope. After establishing your categories, you spend against what you have allocated in each area.

Be careful not to simply track what you have spent. That is not budgeting but rather recordkeeping. What do I mean by that? Occasionally, when I ask people if they are on a budget they reply, "Yes, we track our expenses through an app." It's fine that they track their spending in an app, but that's not a budget system. It may help them set their budget amounts more realistically, but it doesn't help them stay within their planned budget.

For a budget system to function, you must be able to answer the question *How much do I have left to spend in each category?* At any time during the month or year, you should be able to review your finances and know how you are doing against what you planned to spend. It's important to say no to items that are not in the budget or would increase your expenses beyond your income level—for example, a bigger house, a new car, or the latest technology.

Let me illustrate. Assume the amount budgeted for auto repairs for the year is $2,000. Your car breaks down in March, and the repair costs $750. You pay the bill, and you have $1,250 left in the car repair "envelope." You are still on budget for the year. Or what if you budget $500 per month for utilities, but during an unusually cold February, you spend $600? You are over budget that month, but you won't know if you're over or under the total amount in your budget for this category until the end of the year. The spring and summer months may not require as much electricity as you planned, so you may find yourself right on budget.

You may be thinking, "Russ, how can I do that? Spend $600 when I only budgeted $500?" This is where the second key principle comes in.

No system will work without cash on hand.

If you're trying to stay on budget and live paycheck to paycheck, it will not work out. Why? Because *some expenses aren't linear*—they don't necessarily occur in the exact month you planned for them or when you just got paid. A great clothing sale may fall at the same time one of your children gets sick, or the car may break down in the coldest month, so your utility bill spikes. You can cover these expenses and still be on budget if you have cash in reserve to get you started. I've never seen a person who can stay on a budget system if he or she is living paycheck to paycheck!

AN *AHA* MOMENT: MONTHLY VERSUS NONMONTHLY EXPENSES

Differentiating between *monthly* and *nonmonthly* expenses is critical for your budget to work. As a matter of fact, I would go so far as to say that this is the one key for a budget to work. Julie and I have seen this play out over the years as people have said, "Wow, now I get it. This concept has finally allowed us to make a budget work." Why do they say that? What is the great aha breakthrough for them? Let's unpack it together.

Living Expenses

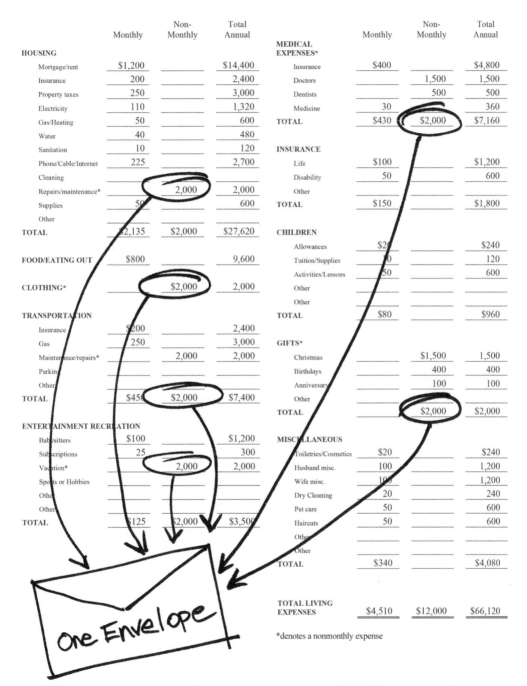

HOUSING	Monthly	Non-Monthly	Total Annual
Mortgage/rent	$1,200		$14,400
Insurance	200		2,400
Property taxes	250		3,000
Electricity	110		1,320
Gas/Heating	50		600
Water	40		480
Sanitation	10		120
Phone/Cable/Internet	225		2,700
Cleaning			
Repairs/maintenance*		2,000	2,000
Supplies	50		600
Other			
TOTAL	2,135	$2,000	$27,620
FOOD/EATING OUT	$800		9,600
CLOTHING*		$2,000	2,000
TRANSPORTATION			
Insurance	$200		2,400
Gas	250		3,000
Maintenance/repairs*		2,000	2,000
Parking			
Other			
TOTAL	$450	$2,000	$7,400
ENTERTAINMENT RECREATION			
Baby-sitters	$100		$1,200
Subscriptions	25		300
Vacation*		2,000	2,000
Sports or Hobbies			
Other			
Other			
TOTAL	$125	$2,000	$3,500

MEDICAL EXPENSES*	Monthly	Non-Monthly	Total Annual
Insurance	$400		$4,800
Doctors		1,500	1,500
Dentists		500	500
Medicine	30		360
TOTAL	$430	$2,000	$7,160
INSURANCE			
Life	$100		$1,200
Disability	50		600
Other			
TOTAL	$150		$1,800
CHILDREN			
Allowances	$20		$240
Tuition/Supplies	10		120
Activities/Lessons	50		600
Other			
Other			
TOTAL	$80		$960
GIFTS*			
Christmas		$1,500	1,500
Birthdays		400	400
Anniversary		100	100
Other			
TOTAL		$2,000	$2,000
MISCELLANEOUS			
Toiletries/Cosmetics	$20		$240
Husband misc.	100		1,200
Wife misc.	100		1,200
Dry Cleaning	20		240
Pet care	50		600
Haircuts	50		600
Other			
Other			
TOTAL	$340		$4,080
TOTAL LIVING EXPENSES	$4,510	$12,000	$66,120

*denotes a nonmonthly expense

One Envelope

Some expense categories occur monthly such as a house payment, gas for the car, groceries, and utility bills. It is appropriate to budget for these monthly. However, other expenses do not typically occur every month and must be budgeted differently. These nonmonthly categories—such as clothes, vacation, gifts, home repairs, auto repairs and fees, or medical expenses—can all be combined in one big "envelope" together. For this category, you don't have to fund the entire year's budget amount in January, but you will need to put in some extra cash to get started (as we mentioned previously in principle 2) and add to it monthly. Having cash on hand to cover these expenses if they occur early in the year will allow your budget to work versus giving up on your budget in February when several of these expenses could occur at the same time.

There may be other categories that are not monthly—such as life insurance, children's summer activities, and pet costs—but for most people, the six biggest nonmonthly categories are auto repair, home repair and maintenance, medical copays, gifts, vacations, and clothing. If you have other nonmonthly categories in your living expenses from chapter 6, then add them to this envelope. Let's look at an example of how the nonmonthly expenses work in your budget.

For simplified numbers, let's say you allocate $2,000 annually to each of the six biggest nonmonthly budget categories ($12,000 total), which is $167 per month for each category and about $1,000 total per month for all categories. As we know, these expenses do not typically happen monthly. Instead, they occur unexpectedly (the car breaks down or the kids get sick) or only once or twice a year, such as a family vacation. This is why you must have some cash in the nonmonthly account to begin the year. If you begin with $1,500 and then add the $1,000 per month needed to fund the categories for the year, then you won't give up on your budget if a category expense exceeds the monthly allocation.

For instance, if in January your car needs a repair for $600, your child has medical expenses of $300, you purchase a wedding gift for $100, and take advantage of a clothing sale for $400, then you can cover all these costs and not blow your budget. For the year, you still have $1,400 ($2,000 - $600) left for auto repairs and maintenance, $1,700 ($2,000 - $300) for medical expenses, $1,900 ($2,000 - $100) for gifts, and $1,600 ($2,000 - $400) for clothes. You are still on budget even though you spent $1,400 while only putting in $1,000 because you had the initial cash deposit of $1,500. At the end of the year, you should have your original seed money of $1,500 left in the account, which can serve as the initial funding for the next year's nonmonthly expenses account.

I've found that by making this designation of nonmonthly expenses, people can stretch their vacation, clothing, and gift dollars further by planning ahead and taking advantage of sales. A month-to-month or paycheck-to-paycheck system doesn't allow for that.

The nonmonthly distinction is also important because these expenses are typically the ones where people overspend. Therefore, controlling them will help you stay on track. Monthly expenses such as utilities, mortgage payments, gas for the car, and groceries are usually about the same each month, and therefore, you won't typically overspend on them.

ADDITIONAL TECHNIQUES

Never use credit cards for monthly items. Pay monthly expenses with cash, checks, or debit cards. The only way you'll know if you're on budget with these expenses is if you pay them monthly. If you don't pay for a monthly expense when it is due, then how can you know how you are doing against your budgeted amount?

I've been confronted many times on the recommendation not to use credit cards for monthly expenses. People are concerned about giving up the reward points that they earn on their credit card, or they ask me about the fraud danger of using debit cards. I understand these issues, but I firmly believe that being current month to month and making sure you are on budget are more important in the long run. I do allow for credit card use for nonmonthly or annual expenses, such as online purchases or annual membership fees.

Choose a budget system that is simple. Most systems that fail are too complicated to be sustainable. Although it seems like a good idea to keep track of every dime spent on drinks, nail polish, or a sleeve of golf balls, it is probably not sustainable in the long run. You may choose to write everything down at first in order to establish realistic expense amounts, but don't plan to do that long term. Julie and I have found that if we set realistic budget amounts, then we only need to go back and get into the details if we have overspent in a category. And since we're aware of how much is left each month, then we can usually adjust our spending accordingly and do not have to track every detail.

As we mentioned in the last chapter, there are some great tools online that can help you set up and track your budget.

Assign responsibility. To make a budget system work, it's ideal to assign each expense item to the person who is most likely to deal with that expense. For example, it's more convenient for Julie to buy groceries than me, so she keeps track of the grocery money. I pay the utilities and various insurances. We both pay for gasoline and haircuts, so we divide those categories accordingly.

Use one account for married couples—no "his" and "hers." Even if you choose to use multiple accounts for your budget system, remember that the money (in total) belongs to both of you. Julie and I find that having one account from which we both pay bills works best. This way, if she spends something for me (gas for my car) or I pick up groceries on my way home, then we can simply make a journal entry to transfer funds to the appropriate person. We don't have to physically move money from one person to the other, since the funds are all coming out of the same account.

COMMON BUDGET QUESTIONS

Can I start using a budget system anytime during the year?
Although it's easiest to start a budget at the beginning of a calendar year, you can start anytime. Regardless of when you start, you will go through the same process to determine the calendar year amounts and then allocate them monthly. For the annual amounts, you will deduct what you've already spent to that point in the year, and you will prorate the remaining amounts for the remainder of the year.

What if I don't have a set salary because I work on commission or do freelance work?
If you have a variable income, you can begin by putting more money into your savings. You can then deposit your variable checks into your savings account and, in essence, salary yourself out of the savings account each month. In other words, you put yourself on a set salary each month, thus removing the monthly variability. You still have to earn a certain total income annually to cover your expenses (living, giving, taxes, and debt payments), but paying yourself a fixed salary should make budgeting easier and less stressful.

Even if you're on a salary, you may want to deposit paychecks into a savings account and pay yourself each month versus trying to figure what to pay from the paycheck on the first and the fifteenth. In other words, go to a once-per-month allocation to fund living expenses instead of two times a month.

Should we have only one checking account?

Not necessarily. You need to adapt your system to fit your family. We have found that one account allows for more flexibility and less paperwork for us. You may find that you like to allocate to separate accounts, or you may have a relationship with more than one bank and, as a result, want to have more than one account. You can have as many accounts as you want. Just remember that the more accounts you have, the more minimum balances you may need to maintain.

What if we don't have cash saved to fund the initial nonmonthly envelope?

You need to do whatever is necessary to come up with some savings. As we have already established, it is impossible to make any budget system work without a cash cushion. You may need to sell an asset, work a second job for a period of time, or sacrifice in some area (maybe no vacations for a year) until you have accumulated enough to make the system you choose work. You could even use your income tax refund to get the budget system started. Having at least one month of expenses in cash is enough to get started.

How do I handle items deducted from my paycheck, such as insurance premiums?

Make sure you include these items in your budget as living expenses (chapter 6). A common mistake people make is to forget to include these categories because they are withheld from the gross paycheck. Since the income box is gross, these deducted amounts must go in one of the other boxes to make sure they are accounted for.

What if we overestimate or underestimate our income for the year?

If during the year you see your income is going to be less than you projected, then you need to adjust your living expenses accordingly unless the savings amount is enough to offset the difference. These variations are another good reason to have an annual cushion and not spend all that you make.

Remember, though, that a reduction in income isn't usually dollar for dollar. If your income goes down $1, for instance, the reduction is really only a percentage of that, depending on your effective tax rate (ETR). For example, if your ETR is 20 percent, your taxes will go down $0.20 on every dollar, so your living expenses would only need to be reduced by $0.80.

If your income is more than projected, great! Just don't spend more than 80 percent of the increase, or you will be in trouble when it comes to paying your annual taxes. Also, you may move into a higher tax bracket, so check with your accountant before you make spending plans.

If your income goes up, you can always add that increase to your charitable giving or savings. Don't automatically opt for a more opulent lifestyle. As we will see in the next chapter, if you always increase living expenses as your income goes up, then it will be more difficult to experience financial freedom and have a chance at financial independence.

What if I'm running out of money before the end of the month?

There are only two possibilities: Either you don't have realistic amounts allocated for expenses and need to increase them, or you have set realistic amounts and just aren't following them. In either case, you need to track the details to see exactly where your money is going so that you can either adjust the funds allocated or cut back on your spending.

What are some of the major budget breakers to watch for?

Budget breakers are generally found among discretionary, nonmonthly budget items. These items are primarily gifts, clothing, vacations, and house furnishings.

It's interesting to note that the nondiscretionary items (fixed expenses such as utilities, mortgage, and gas for vehicles) very seldom are the culprits. It's also interesting that most expenses in the budget are fixed. So the key to avoiding budget breakers is to control the few unfixed expenses that tend to blow the budget. However, if your fixed expenses are too high—perhaps you live in a house that is too much for your income or have car payments that are too high—they will contribute to your budget problems.

Is there an amount that is too much for Christians to have and use for living expenses?

As with many areas of the Christian life, it would be much easier if there were definitive answers, but there is no clear answer to this question. God allows us a great deal of freedom in the lifestyle area. He only gives us these definitive boundaries: Spend less than you make and be content (1 Timothy 6:8), give to the Lord (Luke 6:38), pay the lender (Proverbs 22:7), and pay your taxes (Romans 13:7). Once we do these things, the amount left over is ours to do with as the Lord leads. Maybe we should give more. Maybe we should take more family vacations. These decisions are between God and you. As long as you seek His direction and wisdom and are tuned in to His desires, you have freedom in this area.

It is important to make the lifestyle decisions that work best for you, your family, and your current station in life and know that they may need to be adjusted. You may strive for a simpler lifestyle, but someone in the world will probably always have a simpler one. You may strive to elevate your lifestyle, but someone in the world likely has a higher standard of living. The best answer and choice is simply to walk with God daily and seek contentment.

Accountability in this area will also help make sure you're on track. What do I mean by accountability? Having someone in your life who will be honest regarding your budget may provide some extra insight. On our own, we can justify any amount as "needed" in an expense category, so it can be helpful to have someone periodically check our thinking for realism and balance. Julie and I have such a person in our lives who helps us keep a good balance between giving, living expenses, and savings.

What About You?

Take your living expense sheet on page 63. First, assign responsibility by determining who in your family will monitor each category. Second, determine the nonmonthly categories for your budget. Third, make sure you have cash in the system. And finally, remember that of the first four boxes (giving, taxes, debt, and living expenses) this is the *only* box you need to manage actively. The others are predetermined. If you stay within your living expenses budget, then you will find yourself with positive savings in box 5, and you will be on the way to financial freedom.

8

THE FORMULA

I did not recognize the number as I answered my cell phone one evening. "Hello, this is Russ," I said.

"Hi Russ, this is Peter," said the voice on the other end. "I hate to call you at night, but I wanted to make sure I caught you, and I only had your cell number. I hope you don't mind."

"No worries. How did you get my number?"

"My friend Rob gave it to me. He thought you might be able to help me."

"Well, I hope Rob is right." I commented, sensing the anxiety and reservation in Peter's voice. "What's on your mind?"

"I was laid off last Friday from the company I have been with for 20 years. I have had a good income over the years; my wife and I have educated three children and paid for two weddings. We have a pretty good chunk in our 401(k), and I will get a six-month severance package. My concern is not knowing if I will have enough for retirement. I am 50 years old, and we still have a mortgage on our home along with some other miscellaneous debt. You know it is hard to pay for college and weddings with cash," said Peter as he laughed.

"I agree with you on that," I interjected. "Those are some pretty hefty cash needs. Sounds like you all have had a lot going on. Anything else on your mind?"

"I guess the biggest unknown is what I will be able to make in my next job," said Peter as he sighed. "It is highly unlikely I will continue to earn what I have been making. And I just don't know what I should plan for income-wise in a new job after my severance terminates. Rob said you have some sort of formula that might help me. If so, I'm all ears."

"Well, Peter, I do have a formula," I said, chuckling. "Why don't we find a time for you and your wife to come by the house, and we'll take a look at the formula and determine some figures for you. You will need to bring a list of your living expenses. They are the key to unlocking the answer to your question."

"Sounds great," Peter said, sounding more hopeful. "I really do want to get this figured out."

A COMMON PROBLEM

Over the years, I have found that most people do not know how much they need to earn to support their lifestyle. What they actually need to know is the *minimum* amount they must make to avoid overspending and to ensure box 5 (savings) is positive.

A pay cut or job loss like Peter's will force the issue to the forefront. As people look for another job or try to determine if they can live on a reduced income, they realize they need to be clear on exactly how much they need to earn at a minimum to break even.

THE FORMULA

The way to determine your minimum income needed is simply to take your living expenses total (box 4) and divide by one minus the total of your giving percentage and effective tax rate. If you have any debt in box 3 (debt), then you would need to add your annual minimum debt payment to your annual living expense number to determine the numerator (number above the line) in this equation.

$$\frac{\text{Your Box} \, ④ + \text{Box} \, ③}{1 - (\text{Your Giving} \, \% + \text{Your ETR})} = \text{Income Needed}$$

That is all there is to it. But maybe you were not a math major (like I was), and you thought you were finished with formulas when you graduated from high school. I realize formulas, equations, and numbers freak a lot of people out, so in keeping with our theme of simplicity, let's unpack the formula one step at a time and see if we can help you determine your minimum income needed.

Step 1: *The numerator.* Living expenses drive everything, which is why we spent so much time in the previous chapters focusing on how to determine realistic living expenses and how to control them. The larger the living expense number, the more you will need to earn in the income box to have a positive amount in box 5 (savings) and the harder it will be to have financial freedom. Debt in box 3 will only exacerbate the problem and make the numerator larger. Peter had this issue.

Step 2: *The denominator.* This is the number below the line. The reason for the parenthesis is that you need to add your giving percentage to your effective tax rate (ETR) *before* subtracting from one. For example, if your giving percentage in box 1 (giving) is a tithe or 10 percent and your ETR is 15 percent, then 25 percent is in the parentheses. One minus 25 percent (or .25) is .75. The denominator will always be less than one.

Living expenses are the key in this formula because the more expensive the lifestyle, the higher your income needs to be and more of your income is taxed at the higher marginal rate. Remember that in chapter 4 we discussed the difference between marginal and effective tax brackets. More money taxed at the higher marginal rate pushes your ETR higher. The higher your ETR, the lower the denominator. The lower the denominator, the higher the amount you need to earn.

Illustration

Let's look at what happens to the income needed as your living expenses increase. If your living expenses are $50,000, if your ETR is 15 percent, and if you tithe 10 percent, then you would need to make $66,667 to break even. You would have no savings, but you could give, pay your taxes, and live. (For this illustration, we are assuming the "living expenses" numerator includes minimum annual debt payments from box 3.) If living expenses go up $10,000 ($60,000 total), then the income needed rises to $82,200. So to increase your lifestyle by $10,000, you must earn $15,533 more (55 percent more than the spending increase). Wow!

Part of the reason for the increased income needed is the fact that as more of your income is taxed at higher marginal rates, the ETR goes up. In this case, it increases from 15 percent to 17 percent. The ETR cannot stay the same as your income goes up. That tax increase alone raises the amount you need to make from $80,000 to $82,200. So you have a couple of things going on here that make your income needed increase significantly. You have to not only fund the increasing living expenses with after-tax dollars but also earn more money, as you have fewer after-tax dollars as your ETR increases.

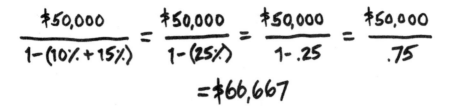

$$\frac{\$50{,}000}{1-(10\%+15\%)} = \frac{\$50{,}000}{1-(25\%)} = \frac{\$50{,}000}{1-.25} = \frac{\$50{,}000}{.75}$$

$$= \$66{,}667$$

$$\frac{\$60{,}000}{1-(10\%+17\%)} = \frac{\$60{,}000}{1-(27\%)} = \frac{\$60{,}000}{1-.27} = \frac{\$60{,}000}{.73}$$

$$= \$82{,}200 \ @ \ 17\% \ ETR$$

$$= \$80{,}000 \ @ \ 15\% \ ETR$$

Look what happens if your living expenses increase to $80,000. The $30,000 increase causes you to have to earn $114,300, or $47,600 more, which is a 59 percent increase in income (from $66,667 to $114,300) over the spending increase. The amount you need to earn will continue to increase percentagewise due to the increasing ETR. If your living expenses increase to $100,000, or a $50,000 increase over where you started, then you would need to make $82,600 more in minimum income or a 65 percent increase in income beyond the spending increase. Another way to look at this is when your living expenses double (from $50,000 to $100,000) then your income needs to more than double. You cannot go from $66,667 to $133,334. You must now earn $149,250!

The amount of earnings needed has grown from 55 percent ($10,000 living expense increase) to 65 percent ($50,000 increase in living expense) over the increased living expenses, and it will continue to grow as your living expenses rise. This is why it is so important to control your lifestyle and make sure you are in the process of taking box 3 (debt) to zero by paying off all consumer debt.

$$\frac{\$80,000}{1-(10\%+20\%)} = \frac{\$80,000}{1-(30\%)} = \frac{\$80,000}{1-.30} = \frac{\$80,000}{.70}$$

$$= \$114,300$$

$$\frac{\$100,000}{1-(10\%+23\%)} = \frac{\$100,000}{1-(33\%)} = \frac{\$100,000}{1-.33} = \frac{\$100,000}{.67}$$

$$= \$149,250$$

BACK TO PETER

As I prepared to meet with Peter, I already knew that our discussion would primarily focus on his living expenses, which likely would be driven to a large degree by his current home expenses. He had probably purchased the home on his current income, expecting it to continue. The more expensive the home, the larger the mortgage and the higher the real estate taxes, insurance, and utilities, not to mention the higher cost for upkeep. Most of our living expenses are driven by our home purchase decision, which is why the home mortgage is part of living expenses and not debt. I suspected that, as with most people, Peter had a large mortgage, which would drive up his living expenses and in turn, drive up his income needed making it difficult for him to find a new, comparable job. I have found that people typically get ahead of themselves with too much house too soon. This decision makes their current income needed quite high, making it harder to spend less than they make and reducing their options if their income decreases. Stress increases and peace of mind decreases. The higher the lifestyle expenses, the harder it is to be financially free and have options to take a lower-paying job or transition to something less stressful.

Looking back at our illustration, you can see that it is much easier for people to have options if they only need to make $66,667 instead of $149,250. I would encourage you, as you strive to be financially free, to be careful of making decisions that drive up your living expenses—first and foremost your home decision but also how and where you vacation, what kind of cars you drive, and so on. Remember, living expenses drive everything!

What About You?

So now it is your turn to work the formula. Want to know your minimum income needed? Add your numbers from box 4 (living expenses) and box 3 (debt) and divide by one minus the total of your box 1 (giving) percentage and box 2 (tax) percentage. It is always good to have an idea of the minimum income you need. Complete the following equation to find the minimum income needed to meet your current expenses.

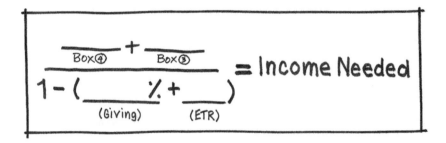

If you earn more than the minimum income needed, then you have a savings amount available to invest. The amount available to invest is the amount you earn over your minimum income needed minus your giving percentage and effective tax rate percentage. For example, if your minimum income needed is $65,000 and you earn $75,000 then you have an excess of $10,000. Take that amount and subtract your giving percentage (let's say 10 percent or $1,000) and your effective tax rate (let's say 15 percent or $1,500) and you have $7,500 available in savings to invest.

9

INVESTMENTS 101

Julie and I were heading into a restaurant for dinner when I heard, "Hey, Mr. Crosson." I turned around to see my neighbor's daughter. I reached out my hand and said, "Hi Lauren. Good to see you! How are you doing?"

"I'm doing well, and I'm so glad I ran into you guys. I just took a new job, and I'm trying to determine what to do about my benefits and have some questions on investing."

"Congratulations on the new job! What is the main question on your mind?" I asked.

"My new company matches 401(k) contributions dollar for dollar up to the first 3 percent of my earnings, and then the match is 50 percent on the dollar on the next 3 percent," Lauren shared.

Interrupting to clarify, I asked, "So you can get a max 4.5 percent match? Is that what I'm hearing?"

"That's right," Lauren said. "I don't know if I should select a regular 401(k) or a Roth 401(k). I'm also thinking I would like to invest in some real estate with some of my savings. It seems that real estate is the way to go for investing."

"Well, Lauren, that may or may not be the case," I interjected. "Real estate is a nonliquid investment and usually something that people invest in after they have taken some other investment steps first. Do you mind if I ask you some questions?"

"Sure. Go ahead," said Lauren agreeably. "Fire away. I really want to make the right decisions with these benefits."

"Okay. You asked for it," I said, chuckling. "Do you know what your annual savings amount will be on your new salary? How much cash do you currently have in the bank? Are you planning to buy a different house anytime soon? How old is your car? Do you have any major purchases coming up in the next couple of years? Is your current lifestyle comfortable, or are some categories too tight? Do you have any debt other than your home mortgage? Do you feel good about your current charitable giving level?"

I could have asked more questions, but you get the point. What most people think is an investment issue really is a much larger question. The first question is the most important. Do you have savings to invest? In other words, is box 5 (savings) positive? I have purposefully written the book to this point to help you determine if you have positive margin (are you spending less than you make each year?). If the income box minus boxes 1, 2, 3, and 4 (giving, taxes, debt, and living expenses) is a positive number, then you can begin to think about investing.

Unfortunately, since most people don't know what is in each box, they don't know if they have margin. It is common for me to meet with someone who has $80,000 in their 401(k) but who also has $80,000 in credit card debt. They have essentially been borrowing on credit cards to fund retirement. This is why it is paramount to build your plan in the order we have discussed. Only after you fill in boxes 1, 2, 3, and 4 (giving, taxes, debt, and living expenses) will you know if you have savings in box 5. If you have savings, then you can begin to think about what to do with that money. How to invest the savings is determined by the answers to the other questions I asked Lauren.

THE BIBLE ON INVESTING

Before we unpack some principles and a process around how to invest your money, let's look at two key biblical principles that are the foundation of any investment decision.

Be Wary of "Get Rich Quick" Schemes

Proverbs 21:5 and 28:20 say that "steady plodding brings prosperity" and that "he who makes haste to be rich will not go unpunished," respectively. Don't chase unrealistic investment returns. If it sounds too good to be true, then it probably is. Stick with tried and true investment vehicles (stocks, bonds, cash, real estate, gold, etc.), and seek out highly recommended and trustworthy advisors with whom you have common values. Proverbs 15:22 says, "Without consultation, plans are frustrated, but with many counselors they succeed."

Diversify Your Investments

Ecclesiastes 11:1-2 makes it clear that we do not know what misfortune may come or what economic cycles may occur, so we are to invest in various tried and true investment vehicles to *preserve* and *grow* our wealth by compounding through whatever happens in the various economic cycles.

People build wealth by spending less than they make and preserving and growing their wealth with diversified investments. Many people get this mixed up. They spend more than they make and think that if they can somehow make the "right investment," with a home-run return then they will be set. In all the years I have been advising people, I have never seen anyone make their wealth through extraordinary investment returns. They accumulated wealth by working hard, spending less than they made, and investing conservatively letting the magic of compounding work for them

I have, on the other hand, seen people lose what they had accumulated by making unwise, aggressive investment decisions. The saddest situation was a man who had accumulated $60 million, and when he died, he left his wife penniless. Unfortunately, he did not pay off his debt and made risky investments.

How Much Do You Actually Have to Invest?

I cannot reiterate enough how important it is to take your income minus boxes 1, 2, 3, and 4 (giving, taxes, debt, and living expenses) to determine your actual savings number, which will show you how much you have available to invest. Often, what happens is that people set their tax withholdings too high and some of their savings is accumulating in the tax box and will come back in the form of a tax refund. Or they default to funding the 401(k) to the max (in Lauren's case this is beyond the 6 percent employer match level). This money is not available in the savings box. Any earnings on assets, which are part of the income box, are staying in their investment accounts. So people not only do not know what their savings should be but they end up scrambling to survive on their take-home pay.

So let's look at a simple straightforward formula to determine how much money you have available to invest.

1. **Earnings on assets.** Remember, in the income box, we include any earnings from investment assets as part of your income. In most cases, people do not have the earnings come to them, but rather, they are left in the investment account. This process is known as reinvestment and is a good use of money, since it is adding to your personal savings in box 5 and does not get into the spending cycle. In our illustration, it is subtracted because you have already invested it, and it is not available to be used in any other investment.

2. **Overwithheld income taxes.** If you have not set your tax withholdings to match your actual income taxes (box 2) and you usually receive a tax refund, then this number will also be subtracted from your savings (box 5). In essence, the government holds some of your savings, and you get it back in the form of a tax refund. Don't spend it! It is not free money! It is part of your investable savings and should be considered when determining what to do with those savings. Note that if you are one of the rare people who owes taxes and does not receive a refund, then the amount you owe will get first priority on your box 5 (savings) number and reduce the amount you have to invest.

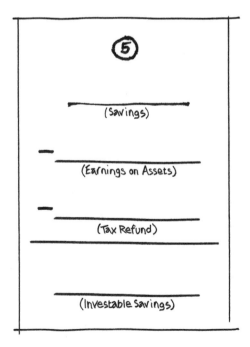

Once you subtract the previous two numbers from your savings number in box 5, then you will have your actual investable savings number. Complete the previous equation to find your investable savings amount.

WHERE TO INVEST

Now that you know exactly how much you have to invest, you can decide what to do with it. That's right; it is *your* decision where that money goes and you have five options that all are legitimate investments. In the graphic that follows you can see the five choices—giving, living expenses, debt, retirement, and personal. Three of these investments are financial capital investments (retirement, personal, and debt payment), one is spiritual capital (giving), and one is social capital (living expenses). To experience financial freedom, you will usually focus on financial capital investments, but all three are important so don't neglect the spiritual and social capital investments. These are very important from an eternal and legacy standpoint.

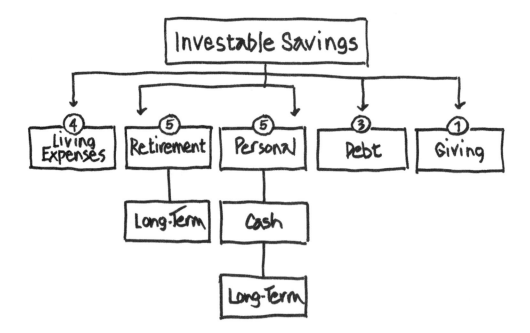

Before I unpack the five investment options for your savings, let me mention that usually people invest in several of these simultaneously. Each year, you may have a different allocation of your savings. One year, you may focus on paying down your debt and building personal savings, and another year, you may add more to your living expenses. Having choices is the cool thing about a positive number in box 5 (savings). You get to decide, and you can alter your decision year to year. I would also encourage you to fund retirement at least to the "match level" if your current employer offers a match option. This is essentially "free money," so while there are still good reasons to forego making these contributions in certain circumstances, this is worth considering. You can carefully review your box 4 (living expenses) to try to take advantage of any matching opportunity. Funding beyond the match level or "overfunding"[1] will depend on other factors noted below. I have found that investing in all five options at different times and in different amounts with a priority on debt repayment and family has been very rewarding and allowed me to experience financial freedom.

The questions I asked Lauren are the same questions you should ask yourself in order to decide how much to invest and where to invest. Now let's look at each of these investment options for your savings:

Invest in retirement or personal funds. In most cases, this decision is the most pressing. Should you invest in retirement funds or personal funds? Asking and answering the right questions will help give you direction.

For example, if you need a car in a year or two, then you cannot buy that car with money in your 401(k), so maybe more of your savings should go into nonretirement investments. If there is no cash on hand to put in the nonmonthly envelope (chapter 7), then perhaps more cash needs to be accumulated personally for that purpose. If you do not have an emergency fund, then more money is needed in a personal savings account or money market fund to avoid the use of credit cards and the high interest rates they carry.

Let me be candid and very direct with you here. This decision is critical to experiencing financial freedom, and yet the majority of people I meet with default to overfunding retirement at the expense of personal investing and debt repayment. A woman Julie and I met recently had $300,000 in retirement and $4,000 in personal cash. She had 75 times as

---

1. For our discussion, overfunding is defined as any amount over the employer match.

much in retirement as in her personal savings. It is almost like it is un-American not to fund your retirement plan to the maximum. Did you notice that Lauren's question was not about whether or not she should fund her 401(k)? Instead, the question was whether to invest in a regular 401(k) or a Roth 401(k).

Unfortunately, most people don't follow the process in this book and don't determine the five uses of money, so they end up with money in their retirement account, but they take on debt for clothing, cars, vacations, and, in some cases, giving. They have not worked through the process to see if they have money to invest. If box 5 (savings) is positive, then you have money to put into a retirement account. We will look at this concept more closely in the next chapter.

There are a myriad of problems with skewing investments toward retirement and not balancing personal investing: A lack of accessible cash restricts your options if something happens (since you have no emergency fund), you do not feel as generous to meet the needs of others, and you end up paying high interest rates on consumer items because you cannot pay cash for them.

Julie and I grasped this concept early on in our marriage, and we have not regretted balancing our investments in retirement and personal savings throughout the years. Some years, we did not even fund retirement in order to replenish our cash reserves, pay for college education, or purchase a car. You may be thinking, "Are you sure you are a financial advisor!? Don't you understand compounding and the employer match?" I do understand it, but let me reiterate that the issue is not so much where you invest but actually having the money to invest. If you have positive savings, then investing in your retirement, at least to the match level, is a wise option. If you do not have a positive number in box 5 (savings), then you need to revisit box 4 (living expenses) and reduce them in order to have savings to invest. What freedom do you have if you have $50,000 in retirement but $40,000 in credit card debt and car loans? Unfortunately, I have seen this scenario far too often!

Pay down debt in box 3. With this investment, you not only earn the interest rate you are paying on your debt, which is a risk-free investment return, but as soon as your consumer debt is paid off, you have zero in box 3 (debt) and that is the goal for this box. As a result, you will have more income to allocate to boxes 1 (giving), 4 (living expenses), and 5 (savings), and this accelerates the path to financial freedom.

Increase living expenses. Perhaps you want to invest more in your family and therefore you need more money allocated to the vacation budget one year. I unpack this concept of investing in posterity with spiritual and social capital in my book *Your Life… Well Spent.*

Increase giving in box 1. You decided your current giving amount earlier in the book. If your current giving is less than 10 percent, then you may decide to increase that number to move toward the goal of tithing. Or if you are already giving 10 percent, then you may want to increase it for the following reasons: (1) you are grateful to God, (2) you have enough in retirement for your age, or (3) you are out of debt and you have additional money that is accumulating. Giving is an investment in spiritual capital.

The Actual Investment Vehicle

At this point, you may be wondering where exactly to put your retirement or personal funds. Since you will not need your retirement funds for many years, you should put them in long-term investment vehicles made up of stocks, bonds, real estate, gold, and cash. Your employer probably offers several options for your retirement portfolio, perhaps ranging from income (most conservative) to growth (most aggressive). Since you will not need this money for a while, I would recommend choosing the higher growth, more aggressive option, since these types of investments typically allow for the greatest return over time.

You should invest any personal savings needed in the next two years in short-term investment vehicles with low risk—such as cash, savings accounts, or money market funds. These funds would include your emergency fund and major purchases (car, furniture, etc.). If you have money that is not needed for five years, then you can consider some bonds or income-type investments. If you have monies that you won't need for at least ten years, then you could invest these funds in more long-term investment vehicles similar to your retirement account.

I suggest that you not invest personal monies in nonliquid investments, such as direct real estate ownership, until you have a fair amount of savings that are liquid (a minimum of 12 months of living expenses). Also before you consider these types of investments, you should pay off all personal debt in box 3 and consider paying off your house mortgage as an alternative fixed-income investment. Paying off your mortgage allows you to "earn" whatever interest rate you are paying and is a risk-free return. Without a home mortgage, your living expenses are lower, which means you aren't required to earn as much income and financial freedom is that much closer.

What About You?

Now it is your turn. Go to the "My Plan" chart in the back of the book and look at your number in box 5 (savings). If that number is positive, then ask yourself the question *Am I allocating my savings the way I want to in light of the five potential places I could invest it?* Then go a little deeper. Ask yourself, *Do I have enough money in my personal savings? Do I have car savings? Do I have an emergency fund? Am I tithing? Should I cut back funding retirement to the match level for a season? Should I cut out retirement funding altogether for a couple of years to build up other areas? Do I always get a tax refund? Should I change my withholdings to reduce that refund?*

Let me encourage you by saying that making sure box 5 (savings) is positive[2] is the most important step. God will give you wisdom as you make choices about your savings.

I think it might be helpful to share my real-life example of these options. Julie and I began by accumulating personal savings for emergencies and paying off our debt. Then we simultaneously invested in retirement while putting money toward paying off the house and investing in my business. We also made the decision to stay in the same home instead of buying a larger house and taking on a higher mortgage. Once the house was paid off, we continued to invest in retirement and the business while increasing our long-term, personal investments. We also have been able to increase our giving along the way. Let me encourage you by saying that the difficult decisions or sacrifices you may have to make now to have positive savings in box 5 will provide freedom in the future. Trust me; looking back, it has been worth the sacrifices we made.

---

2. Percentages of your income to save may vary based on age, but a good goal to start with is to save at least 10%.

10

Don't Be in a Hurry to Quit

I was surprised and glad to see the number on the caller ID on my house phone (yes, we still have one of those) was my youngest son's number.

"Hello, is everything okay?" I inquired, as any dad does when he gets a call from a child away at college.

"Yeah, everything's great!" responded Chad in his typical upbeat voice.

"What's up then? You usually don't call us, especially at this time of night," I said jokingly.

"In my finance class today, we were talking about retirement, and they introduced the idea of a Roth IRA," Chad explained. "It sounds like a great way to invest, and I am thinking I should open one. What do you think?"

"Well, that is a good question, Son," I answered, grinning. "Glad to know you are listening in class! Let me ask you some questions: Do you have three to twelve months of living expenses saved up? Do you have money for your next car? Do you have money saved for a down payment on a house? You do know you will need a place to live when you graduate, right?"

"But Dad!" interrupted Chad. "My professor showed us that if I start now, the compounding will be incredible, and I could have a million dollars by the time I'm 65!"

"I agree; compounding is a great thing when it works in your favor," I said reassuringly. "Your professor is right about that. But there is more to securing your financial future than just putting money in a retirement plan and letting compounding take over. How about the next time you are home, we look at some of the issues that should be considered before you fund your retirement? After all, you are only 21."

"Okay, you are probably right. Sounds like a plan," Chad muttered in a somewhat-resigned tone.

THE PROBLEM

I touched on this briefly in the last chapter as we looked at the five options for investing your savings. For most people, the default is to put money into retirement first at the maximum level possible, whether it is a 401(k), a Roth IRA, or some other form of tax-deferred plan—SEP, 403(b), Keogh, and so on. This money is often withheld from your paycheck, and you don't see it as part of your income. This oversight may not be a problem if you have plenty of savings and can afford to fund retirement. Unfortunately, my observation is that most people don't have enough in annual savings to invest in retirement at the level they are contributing, if at all.

Let's look at some signs that you may not have enough in box 5 (savings) to fund retirement at the maximum level (remember the goal at a minimum is to take advantage of the employer match).

There is debt in box 3, and it is not being reduced. If you have a number in box 3 (debt) and that number is growing or not decreasing, then that may show you do not have enough money in box 5 (savings) to maximize retirement funding right now. It means that in all likelihood, you are borrowing money in order to fund retirement at your current level. If you don't have margin, then you are counting on your retirement investment returns to outperform the cost of the consumer and credit card debt you are carrying. You have not only made a financial bet but given yourself the stress of the debt, which is also a burden.

You do not have an emergency fund or cash to fund your nonmonthly expenses. I suggest you have three to twelve months of living expenses in a personal savings account for emergencies. The money in your retirement account is not accessible if the car breaks down or you need a new air-conditioning unit. As we discussed in chapter 7, having some cash available for unpredictable, nonmonthly expenses or even unplanned spikes in monthly expenses is crucial. The cash also provides an emergency fund in case your income unexpectedly decreases or you lose your job. I caution you not to overfund retirement at the expense of your personal savings.

Recently, a tornado came through our property. The house was spared, but many trees weren't. The tree company estimates it will cost $10,500 to clean everything up, and insurance does not cover the expense because the house was not damaged. That money has to come from my emergency fund. Life is unpredictable, and we must be financially prepared for the unexpected.

Your budget system is not working. As we unpacked earlier, any budget system requires cash. The following are symptoms that show that money should not be invested in retirement: There is no cash to prime the nonmonthly categories, you cannot buy back-to-school supplies without stress, or you cannot repair the car without blowing your budget. You can't buy kids' socks, take a family vacation, or buy new cars with retirement money.

You are not paying cash for cars. Inevitably, you will need to purchase a new car, and if you do not have savings in a new car fund, then you will be forced to borrow from a lender and take on debt. As we saw in chapter 8, debt increases the numerator in our formula driving up the amount of income you need to earn, thus making your financial options and freedom more elusive.

You are paying mortgage insurance. If you did not put down 20 percent on your home or have not accumulated 20 percent to put down, then you are (or will be) paying monthly mortgage insurance. The mortgage insurance premium and the higher mortgage debt amount will work against whatever you are accumulating in your retirement plan.

In summary, be careful not to default to overfunding retirement at the expense of the other four investment options. Doing all of them over time is the ultimate key to financial freedom.

Pace of Life

The concept of retirement, as we know it today, was derived from the Social Security Act of 1935. Under pressure, Franklin D. Roosevelt enacted this legislation to create public pensions that would encourage older workers to retire and create employment for younger workers. In the 1940s and 1950s, private company pensions became the norm due to favorable tax laws.

Since then, pensions and retirement plans have been emphasized at the expense of personal investing and balancing life. Today, most people are in a hurry to quit work in order to enjoy life, so they begin funding retirement to the max as soon as they start working, feeling like it is nonnegotiable. Unfortunately, this mind-set accelerates the pace of life and may cause people to focus on the long term instead of enjoying the journey and putting stress on the uses of money diagram we have been discussing. Too much money in retirement too soon makes it more difficult to spend less than you make.

Don't get me wrong. I am not against retirement savings. Retirement funding just needs to be kept in balance, in the proper sequence, and the proper amount. Let's walk through the steps you can take to invest wisely and enjoy financial freedom along the way.

SEQUENTIAL INVESTING

The issue is not funding retirement but rather the timing and amount. If you want to experience financial freedom, it is best to invest your savings in the following sequence:[1]

---

1. Steps 1 and 2 will need to be done simultaneously. It is impossible to take *all* your cash to pay off debt and also accumulate cash. You will need to do both a little at a time. Since cash is essential for a budget to work, you may need to start with step 2: Save for a couple of months, use cash to pay off the debt in step 1, and then go back and continue to build on step 2.

Step 1: *Pay off all personal debt in box 3.* As we discussed previously, paying off consumer debt allows you to avoid paying high interest rates, which is the same as earning those rates of return. If your credit card's interest rate is 12 percent and you pay it off, then you just earned the 12 percent, since you no longer have to pay on it. Also once the debt box is zero, then you have more money going into box 5 (savings), which gives you more options.

Step 2: *Accumulate three to twelve months of living expenses in a short-term savings account.* There are two positive impacts of having these funds in savings. First, you have cash to make your budget work. Second, you have cash available to handle emergencies and avoid the use of consumer debt.

Step 3: *Save for major purchases.* Saving for purchases such as a car and house down payment in a short-term savings account will hopefully allow you to avoid the expense of financing a car or paying mortgage insurance by allowing you to put at least 20 percent as a down payment.

Step 4: *Fund retirement and other long-term goals.* After the other steps are complete, you can begin to fund long-term goals such as retirement, paying off your house mortgage, and making longer-term personal investments—stocks, bonds, and real estate.

Julie and I followed the previous sequence and have no regrets. We will share with our son Chad the sequence of investing and recommend that he needs to accumulate approximately $50,000 in personal funds before he begins to think about retirement. His professor did not explain that personal savings are needed to build a solid financial foundation. The Roth IRA is premature for Chad at this stage of his savings.

You may be thinking that $50,000 is a very large amount of savings. But if you add up three to six months in an emergency fund ($5,000–$10,000), $15,000 to $20,000 to pay cash for a car, and $20,000 to $40,000 to pay 20 percent down on a house, then the funds needed add up quickly. Depending on your taste, $50,000 may not be enough.

I know your employer has a 401(k) match, and I know that is free money. I know it is difficult to turn that down. My hope is that you have enough money in box 5 (savings) to be able to take advantage of the company match. If you have completed steps 1 through 3 or if you have some time before you need to purchase a car or a home, then *simultaneously* investing in retirement while you do steps 1 through 3 would be my recommendation. But if you don't have a positive number in box 5 (savings) or it is not large enough to do steps 1 through 3 *and* fund retirement, then delay retirement funding awhile. Hopefully the motivation to take advantage of the employer match will help you to control living expenses so you have enough savings to invest in steps 1 through 3 *and* retirement simultaneously.

What Julie and I see most of the time are people with a lot of money in retirement, but they still have consumer debt, financed cars, and mortgage interest to pay. Cutting back on funding retirement could help reduce some of these outflows. If your company matches 3 percent, then don't contribute more than that until your personal savings increase. Look at other budget categories, and see if you can cut back on them to fund retirement and take advantage of the company match. In some cases, it may be best to stop funding retirement for a season until you have an emergency fund accumulated.

What About You?

Take your time. I know this is a big issue. Look at your actual savings and then prayerfully decide how to allocate it. Don't be in a hurry to quit working. You don't have to fund every category at once! Balance retirement and personal investing. If you need to change your current retirement withholdings for a season to make some other investments, then have the courage to do so. Remember, as long as box 5 (savings) is positive you will continue to move toward financial freedom regardless of how you allocate it. Enjoy the trip.

11

LIVE ON ONE INCOME

As you have worked through this book to make sure you are spending less than you make and beginning on the path to financial freedom, you have also been reminded of the importance of cash. In the last chapter, I mentioned the goal of accumulating $50,000 in cash for an emergency fund, house down payment, and major purchases, such as vehicles. If you have personal debt, then those numbers should be added to the $50,000. This amount of cash can appear overwhelming and out of reach, but it isn't if you make a commitment to live on one income when you are getting started as a couple.

A few years ago, I was visiting with leaders at Focus on the Family about principles young couples need to understand. They asked, "If you could share one idea with a couple, what would it be?" I responded, "That is easy. If couples would simply practice living on one income and saving the other from the beginning, then it would have incredibly positive consequences on their financial futures."

When Julie and I got married, I was a schoolteacher, and she was a nurse anesthetist. She made twice what I made, but we committed to living on my income and saving her income (after taxes and giving). Although it was difficult to live on one income and the budget was tight, it gave us a solid foundation. We learned that if it is hard early on, then it will get easier later, but if you make it easy on yourself early, then it will get harder later. It is very easy to get in the habit of living on both incomes. Cash flow is plentiful, so there is no need to budget or watch expenses. Vacations, new clothes, and a trendy loft are all within reach on two incomes. But what happens later if one of you loses your job or decides to stay home? It is difficult to cut back your spending to one income and even more difficult if you haven't saved cash or have taken on car loans and credit card debt. Your cash flow is strained because you did not store up cash when you had a golden opportunity to do so.

You may always plan to have two incomes, but there will never be a time in your life when your expenses are as low as they are early in your relationship. Life—children, moves, furnishing a home—has a way of increasing your expenses. The best time to maximize your savings is when you first start your journey. Even if you continue to have two incomes, storing up significant cash early on gives you options, plus it allows you to take the sequential investment steps in chapter 10, which will put you on the path to financial freedom.

GETTING TO $50,000

Let's look at how quickly you can get to the goal of $50,000 if you practice living on one income. In our illustration, each person earns $40,000 right out of college. If you are committed to living on one income, then the funds for living expenses, giving, taxes, and debt payment are coming from $40,000, leaving the other $40,000 untouched except for taxes and giving. If we use 10 percent for giving and an effective tax rate (ETR) of 15 percent, that means 25 percent of the second $40,000 goes to those two boxes, leaving 75 percent or $30,000 to savings (box 5). Do that for two years, and you have $60,000 in savings. You then have funds to buy a car, put 20 percent down on a house, and avoid credit card debt. It puts you on a solid financial foundation.

MOTIVATIONS TO PRACTICE THIS PRINCIPLE

Still not convinced you should make it difficult on yourself and live on one income when you have two? Perhaps the following reasons will be motivators. Living on one income gives you the following benefits:

1. It allows you to get box 3 (debt) to *zero* more quickly. Once this box is zero, you have more cash, which means more options for retirement savings, personal savings, better lifestyle, and so on. My middle son, Reed, used the second income to pay off his wife's student loan debt in the first year of their marriage, which took box 3 to zero for them.

2. It gives you the cash to help make a budget work (chapter 7).

3. It gives you more cash for a house down payment. As we have seen, your home mortgage and house costs are critical components of living expenses. The larger the down payment, the smaller the mortgage and the better off you will be.

   Let's say you are living off $80,000 (two incomes of $40,000 per year). When you get ready to purchase a home, you don't have money for a 20 percent down payment, so you have the added cost of mortgage insurance and a larger mortgage. But what if you lived on one income for three years and saved $30,000 per year? Then you would have $90,000 saved up and be in a position to buy the home you really want, avoid mortgage insurance, and pay a lower mortgage amount.

4. It allows you to have cash for emergencies and avoid the need to use credit cards when unplanned expenses arise.

5. It gives you the option to eliminate one income should you so choose to do so in the future. You have set your budget to live on one income and save the rest, so if the second income is not there, then you are still on track and don't have to adjust your spending. My experience is that if a couple gets used to living on two incomes, then it is difficult, if not impossible, to adjust to one. Remember, the definition of freedom is having options.

Living on one income and saving the other income can set you up for financial freedom in the future. Financial maturity is forgoing current desires for future rewards and benefits.

I know this concept is not easy to live out. You will most likely look different than your friends who are living on two incomes. You may not be able to take the same elaborate ski trips or drive the same kind of cars or go out to eat every weekend, but the sacrifices you make now will pay off later. I've been there. Julie and I drove old cars, did not have a dining room table for three years while we saved up money, did not go on lavish vacations, and did not eat out very much. I even took my lunch to work every day. But now, fast-forward decades later, and we have financial freedom because we applied this principle and others in this book. Many of our friends who made it look easy and spent haphazardly when they were younger are now struggling with fewer options.

Another saying I like is "The longer-term your perspective, the better your decisions today." I hope you will think long-term and have the courage to exhibit maturity in your financial life by living on one income and saving the rest. It is worth it. And trust me; you won't regret it.

12

GET YOUR
THINKING ON

When my oldest son, Clark, was about three years old, he didn't know how to say, "You made me lose my train of thought." So he would say, "You got my thinkin' off." Unfortunately, many of us have our thinking off regarding money.

As we wrap up this book on making your money management simple, I want to share a couple of principles that have helped Julie and me think about our money, gain perspective, be content, experience balance in our lives, and be wise stewards. I am guessing that as you worked through this book, you had the thought, maybe more than once, that if you had a larger salary or more investments or bigger bonuses, then your money would be simple. I know these thoughts because I have them too. It is easy to look around and assume that someone else has more or has it easier than you. As we have mentioned, the tendency is to get out of balance and seek more versus being content with your lot in life. The antidote for me when I am feeling this way is to "get my thinking on." Let me share the origin of the first principle.

FAMILY VACATION

Julie and I had been married one year when we put everything we owned in a U-Haul and moved from Kansas to Atlanta to begin working for a start-up financial services firm (the company I am still with today). God blessed us with three sons, and as they were growing up, we would load everyone in the car and head back to Kansas to visit grandparents and cousins during the summers. It was a 16- to 24-hour car ride across the country.

During these trips, we began a tradition of getting off the interstate highways and driving the two-lane roads instead of the expressways. We told the boys we wanted them to experience America up close and personal as we stopped at roadside parks, ate at local cafes, and took in the local sights, even stopping at a rodeo along the way once. As we wove through one small town after another on our way to Kansas, I began to notice a familiar pattern.

Often, as we approached a small town, we would see a stately large home, typically nicely manicured, with cattle grazing on 40 to 80 acres of pasture within a white fence. After a few of these large homes, as we moved into the middle of town, we would see smaller homes that were still very nice. Then as we began exiting the town, the houses would get smaller until we crossed the railroad tracks and went by mobile homes before heading to the next town. Then 30 miles down the road, we would come to another town and the same pattern would occur—big homes on acreage, then nice homes with less land, then smaller homes, and then mobile homes. And so it would go all across the country.

Obviously, the folks with the larger homes with the acreage and cattle had more income and financial resources than those on the other side of the tracks in the mobile homes. They might have been the doctors, dentists, lawyers, or business owners in town. Then it dawned on me that in the next town, as the same scenario played out, it was highly unlikely that the wealthy person in that town knew the wealthy person in the next town. Most likely, the knowledge of that person's wealth was limited to that unique small town. Then I thought about Atlanta and other major cities. Every city has certain wealthy people with nice material possessions, but they are not known in other cities. So the principle applies not only in small towns but in large cities as well. I recently read an article about two businessmen who are competing for the most expensive house in their city. One is $193 million, and the other will be $240 million when it is complete. Guess what? You and I will likely never see those homes and only a handful of others will.

THE PRINCIPLE OF LIMITED SPHERE

What is the principle? The principle is that no matter what your income level, where you live, what you drive, or what you wear, only a limited number of people will ever know. Your material lifestyle will only be known by a "limited sphere" of people.

Why does this matter? How should this encourage you as you come to the end of this book? It should help you find contentment to practice spending less than you make regardless of what you make. It should help you not feel the need to catch up or keep up or look a certain way to impress people because only a few will ever know what you have materially. Contentment will help you limit your use of consumer debt, not buy too much house, make wiser financial decisions, and focus on what really matters in life. All these choices will make it easier to have a positive number in box 5 (savings), which will help you experience financial freedom.

This thinking has helped Julie and me when we are tempted to look at what others have or begin to feel discontent where we are. I am reminded that only a few people will ever see my material possessions, so there is no need to get my finances out of balance to impress this limited number of people. It is wiser to live within my income and not long for something bigger, better, or newer. This thinking leads to the second principle—the principle of vocation.

THE PRINCIPLE OF VOCATION

In Proverbs 10:22, we read, "It is the blessing of the LORD that makes rich, and He adds no sorrow to it." And in Deuteronomy 8:16-18, we read that it is the Lord who gives us the ability to make wealth. Income is a function of our work, and what we do vocationally is ordained by God through how He has gifted us. I am always amazed when I read the annual *Parade* magazine issue that shows differing income amounts for people. You have fence builders, garbage collectors, doctors, movie stars, athletes, fitness gurus, gardeners, chefs, business owners, freelance artists, arborists, and the list goes on and on. Incomes range from $15,000 to millions of dollars. Ecclesiastes 9:11 is true: "The race is not to the swift and the battle is not to the warriors, and neither is bread to the wise nor wealth to the discerning nor favor to men of ability." Some make a lot; some make a little.

The person at the edge of town with the white fence and large home has a different vocation and different income than the person on the other side of the tracks in the mobile home. Both have enough to meet their needs because God promises that in Philippians 4:19. The question is, Will they live within their income, whatever that level is, and experience financial freedom? Will they understand the principle of limited sphere and not try to impress people by living beyond their means? Remember the key to financial freedom is not how much you make but rather spending less than you make and doing it for a long time.

You may desire to improve your skills, further your education, or work harder to increase your earnings. That decision is up to you, but the important things are to live within your income (regardless of what it is) and learn to be content.

What About You?

You should have completed the "My Plan" chart by this time and know if you are on your way to financial freedom or if you need to make some adjustments. I hope that this chapter has given you some perspective and encouragement so you can continue to have positive savings regardless of your income level. I hope you have a greater appreciation for the source of your income and can find contentment, recognizing that it is not how much you make but rather spending less than you make that is the key to financial freedom. Maybe it will give you the courage to increase your savings by driving an older car a little longer or staying in a smaller house a few more years. Remember that making difficult sacrifices now will make life easier later.

Let me encourage you by saying that direction determines destination. Even if your savings seem small today, don't lose heart (Galatians 6:9). You are taking the right steps and are on the right path if you are seeking God as you give, save, and spend. As you continue to do *your part* of managing toward a positive savings number and trusting God to do *His part* by taking care of your income, then you will experience financial freedom today and tomorrow.

Conclusion

Age 20　Spend less than you make every year

—Take savings and

— Over time pay off <u>ALL</u> debt and <u>HOME</u>

Age 40　—Don't over fund retirement

— Live on a budget

— Diversify your investments

Age 60　— Be generous

Experience Freedom and
Options as You Grow Older

Age 80　Enjoy the Trip!!

My Plan

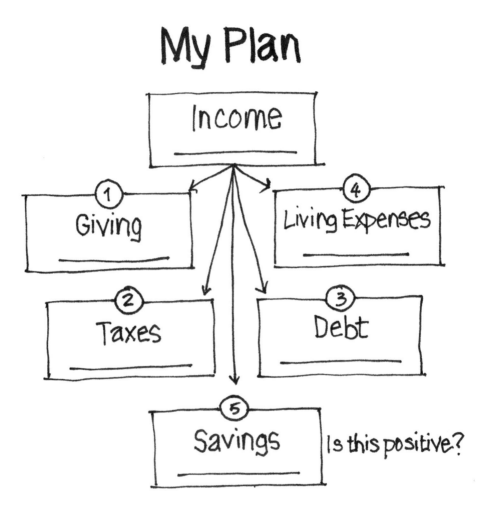

YES: on your way to financial freedom.

NO: what am I going to do to make it positive?

Glossary of Financial Terms

401(k): A retirement plan where an employee can make contributions from his or her paycheck either before or after taxes, depending on the options offered in the plan.

403(b): A retirement plan offered by public schools and certain tax-exempt organizations.

ASSET ALLOCATION: The division of an investment portfolio among asset classes (e.g., stocks, bonds, commodities).

BASIS POINT: The smallest measure used in quoting bond yields. One basis point equals 0.01 percent. Thus 100 basis points equal 1 percent.

BEAR MARKET: Historically defined as a 20 percent decline in the stock market.

BLUE-CHIP STOCK: The stock of a large, financially sound corporation with a strong earnings record.

BOND: Legally binding agreement given to you in exchange for a sum of money that a corporation, state, municipality, or church, for example, agrees to repay to you at a specified maturity date with an agreed amount of interest.

BULL MARKET: A rising stock market. A bull market typically exists when corporate earnings are strong and rising and investors are optimistic about future market performance.

CAPITAL GAIN/LOSS: Difference between total proceeds from the sale of an asset (e.g., real estate, stock, mutual fund, equipment) and its cost basis.

COMMODITIES: A basic good used in commerce that is interchangeable with other units of the same type (e.g., copper, soybeans, crude oil, gold). Commodities are typically used as inputs in the production of other goods or services. You can invest in commodities.

COST BASIS: The tax cost that is typically the original price paid by the buyer for an asset plus reinvested dividends in the case of mutual funds.

DIVIDEND: A payment made by corporations to its shareholders. Corporations usually distribute dividends based on their profits.

DOLLAR-COST AVERAGING: A method of purchasing investments at regular intervals with a fixed amount of dollars regardless of the prevailing prices of the investments. Periodic payments buy more shares when the price is low and fewer shares when it rises.

EXCHANGE-TRADED FUND (ETF): An index-tracking fund that trades on an exchange, enabling it to be bought and sold throughout the day.

FEDERAL FUNDS RATE: The rate banks charge each other for overnight loans. As a key determinant of borrowing costs throughout the economy, the Federal Reserve uses the federal funds rate to manage the economy.

GROWTH INVESTMENTS: Investments that are focused on the growth of an investor's capital.

INCOME AND GROWTH INVESTMENTS: Investments that pursue a balance between growth and income.

INCOME INVESTMENTS: Investments that generate cash income in the form of dividends or interest.

INDEX: A group of securities that is mainly used as a benchmark to measure historical rates of return of broad markets. For example, the Dow Jones Industrial Average is a stock index that consists of 30 blue-chip stocks. The S&P 500 is an index of 500 of the largest US stocks.

INDEX FUND: A passively managed fund that mimics a specified market index, such as the S&P 500.

INDIVIDUAL RETIREMENT ACCOUNT (IRA): An individual investment account that is used to reserve funds for retirement savings. It may include stocks, bonds, and/or mutual funds. There are several types of IRAs including traditional IRAs, Roth IRAs, SIMPLE IRAs, and SEP IRAs.

INFLATION: An increase in the price of goods and services and a fall in the purchasing value of currency.

KEOGH PLAN: A tax-deferred pension plan available to self-employed individuals or unincorporated businesses for retirement purposes.

LARGE-CAP STOCK: A stock of a large company as measured by its market capitalization (number of shares outstanding multiplied by share price).

LIQUID ASSETS: Assets that can easily be converted to cash at their current fair market value.

MARKET CORRECTION: A drop of 10 percent or more in the stock market.

MATCHING CONTRIBUTION: A matching dollar amount contributed by an employer to the retirement savings account—usually a 401(k) plan—of an employee who makes a similar contribution.

MONEY MARKET FUND: A mutual fund that invests in short-term, high-quality, very-liquid debt instruments such as treasury bills.

MUNICIPAL SECURITIES: Bonds issued by state and local government units. The income from these securities is exempt from federal income taxes (also state and local income taxes in some states).

MUTUAL FUND: A fund made up of various securities (e.g., stocks and bonds) and managed by a fund manager. Investors buy shares of the fund rather than owning the individual securities.

NO-LOAD FUND: A mutual fund that does not have a direct sales commission or sales charge.

NONLIQUID ASSETS: Assets that cannot easily be converted to cash without a substantial forfeiture or loss.

PRIME RATE: Interest rate benchmark used by banks in establishing lending rates.

PROSPECTUS: A publication describing securities or investments offered for sale to the public.

QUALIFIED DISTRIBUTIONS: A tax and penalty-free distribution made from a retirement account that must meet certain requirements.

REAL ESTATE INVESTMENT TRUST: A company that owns, operates, or finances income-producing real estate. They are typically traded on major exchanges like common stocks and provide investors with a liquid stake in real estate.

RISK: The possibility of not obtaining the expected return from an investment.

RISK-FREE RATE OF RETURN: The rate of return on an asset that theoretically carries no risk. US Treasury bills are often used to represent this measure.

ROTH IRA: A type of individual retirement account (IRA) that is funded with after-tax dollars. Therefore, the contributions are not tax deductible, but when you start withdrawing funds, the qualified distributions are tax-free.

SAVINGS ACCOUNT: An interest-bearing deposit account held at a bank or another financial institution.

SEP IRA: A simplified employee pension (SEP) is a retirement plan that an employer or self-employed individual can use to provide retirement benefits.

SIMPLE IRA: A Savings Incentive Match Plan for Employees (SIMPLE) retirement plan can be established by most small businesses with 100 or fewer employees to provide retirement savings to its employees.

SMALL-CAP STOCK: The stock of a small company as measured by its market capitalization (number of shares outstanding multiplied by share price).

STOCK: Represents an ownership interest in a corporation.

TREASURY BILL (T-BILL): A debt obligation issued and backed by the US Treasury Department with a maturity of less than one year.

W-2: A required form distributed by employers to employees and the Internal Revenue Service (IRS) at the end of the year. The W-2 form reports an employee's annual wages and the amount of taxes withheld from his or her paycheck.

YIELD: Dividends or interest paid by a security expressed as an annual percentage of the security's current price.

ACKNOWLEDGMENTS

As with any book, many people contribute to its creation. This book is no exception. My longtime assistant, Bonnie Davidson, typed the myriad of changes I continued making to the manuscript while also doing her day job with competence and professionalism. She also put herself into the book and followed its instructions, and when she was finished, she had her plan completed. That encouraged me that we might indeed be onto something with this format.

Malissa Light did a multitude of tasks as she interfaced with Harvest House, provided editorial and proofreading expertise, gathered endorsements, and worked with the artist on the artwork for the book. This book would not have been possible without all her effort.

Robert Niles of Robert Niles Design provided the compelling artwork found in the book and made the "flip chart" concept come alive.

Marshall Potter, a senior financial advisor with Ronald Blue Trust, read the manuscript and provided helpful and pertinent input to make the final product more user-friendly for today's audience.

I am indebted to Ronald Blue Trust for providing a 40-year foundation and forum from which the principles in this book have been proof tested. A special thank-you to the Ronald Blue Trust leadership team members who lead the company day to day and made it possible for me to have the time and platform to pen this book.

Thanks again to Bob Hawkins, Terry Glaspey, and the Harvest House team for believing in this book and making it a reality after I sketched it out in their offices two years ago.

To my lovely bride, Julie, I can only say, "Thank you." You have sat with me in hundreds of meeting with couples and individuals as we shared the concepts in this book and always had keen insights and encouraging words for them and for me. You have been the wind beneath my wings and my fellow co-laborer for four decades in helping folks become financially free. As you said when you read this manuscript and added your helpful comments, "This is just what we tell people when we meet with them." Thanks for making the book better with your comments and making me better because you are in my life.

Finally, I am grateful that the God of the universe is in the freedom business. Not only did He save me and set me free from sin, for which I am eternally grateful, but He also gave me His Word, which contains invaluable wisdom regarding money. Without His Word on this subject, I could not share the one key to financial freedom highlighted in this book. His Word on money is the foundation for people to become financially free.

About the Author

Russ Crosson is executive vice president and chief mission officer of Ronald Blue Trust and executive vice chairman of the board of directors for Thrivent Trust Company. Prior to his current position, Russ served as president and CEO of Ronald Blue & Co. (2002–2017), where he was the second employee hired. From 1999 to 2002, Russ served as executive director of the National Christian Foundation (NCF).

Russ is the author of several books, including *Your Life…Well Spent*, *The Truth About Money Lies*, and *What Makes a Leader Great*. He has also been a featured speaker in many venues, including Promise Keepers, Issachar Summit, and America's Best Hope. He and his wife, Julie, have led seminars around the country on the subjects of money, marriage, and communication. He currently serves on the board of directors for Fellowship of Christian Athletes (FCA).

Russ graduated from Kansas State University with a bachelor's degree in mathematics and a master's degree in education. He and Julie live in Roswell, Georgia, and are active in the teaching and mentoring of young married couples. They have three sons, three daughters-in-law, and six grandchildren.

RonaldBlueTrust™

Wisdom for Wealth. *For Life.*

With nationwide capabilities, Ronald Blue Trust provides wealth management strategies and trust services based on biblical principles to help clients make wise financial decisions, live generously, and leave a lasting legacy. Through a network of 14 branch offices, we serve clients in all 50 states through four distinct divisions and offer services across the wealth spectrum.

Ronald Blue Trust offers many resources on the topics of financial planning, giving, family & life, economy & investments, leadership, and retirement. Some of the wisdom we offer on these subjects comes in the form of books, which include the following titles: *Your Life...Well Spent, The Truth About Money Lies, What Makes a Leader Great,* and *Faces of Generosity.* Please visit www.ronblue.com to view newsletters and videos in our Library, subscribe to our *Insights* blog, and learn more about our services.

BRANCH OFFICES

Ronald Blue Trust's financial professionals serve clients from the following office locations:

Atlanta, GA, Baltimore, MD, Charlotte, NC, Chicago, IL, Greenville, SC, Holland, MI, Houston, TX, Indianapolis, IN, Montgomery, AL, Nashville, TN, Orange County, CA, Orlando, FL, Phoenix, AZ, Seattle, WA

CONTACT

Internet: www.ronblue.com
Mail: 1125 Sanctuary Parkway
    Suite 500
    Alpharetta, GA 30009

Phone: 800-841-0362
Fax: 770-280-6001
E-mail: info@ronblue.com

YOUR LIFE...WELL SPENT

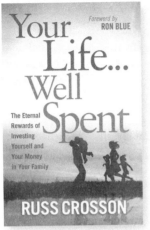

When most Christians think about money, they think about what money can do for them now, *here* in this life.

But attitudes about money have an eternal aspect, and author Russ Crosson, CEO of Ronald Blue & Co. and a highly respected investment advisor, offers a look at how to manage money with eternity in view. Learn the difference between *prosperity*, the accumulation of goods on this earth, and *posterity*, the heritage left to the generations that follow.

Discover a new way of thinking about money, about your life's work—and about how to get a higher return on life itself.

"Without the information in this book, your budget may be balanced but unwise—your bookkeeping may be timely but reflect only temporal values. This is the book to read first, before any others, for the renewing of your financial mind."
Bruce Wilkinson, author of *The Prayer of Jabez*

THE TRUTH ABOUT MONEY LIES

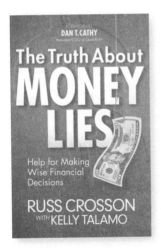

In this important book, Russ teams up with gifted communicator Kelly Talamo to offer the truth about popular money lies that influence the spending decisions of millions of Americans.

Using everyday stories about men and women facing tough financial choices, the authors expose the lies and give truth principles based on the Bible to refute them. For example:

- 10 percent is God's, 90 percent is mine
- I can't afford to give
- My security is in my investments
- My talents and abilities produce my wealth
- The harder I work, the more money I make

You will be better equipped to manage money, make informed financial decisions, and use your money wisely when you replace with biblical truths the common money lies you've been taught.

WHAT MAKES A LEADER GREAT

What makes a good leader? Russ Crosson, author and CEO of Ron Blue & Co., knows—and he learned the hard way: "It's doubtful that anyone can lead effectively until they've been humbled or hurt deeply."

Russ's humbling experience has taught him that leadership success isn't about the leader at all. It's about the mission of the organization, church, business, or even family where the leader serves. It's about who will replace you when you're gone.

Here is a concise, targeted look at what true leadership is, emphasizing its legacy aspect.

Many leadership books are "how-to" or "what to do" books. Here is something different: a *why*-to book that will help you succeed in more important ways than you ever imagined.